PADDINGTON to WEYMOUTH

The Route in the 1950s

Derek Phillips

Irwell Press Ltd.

First published in the United Kingdom in 2012
by Irwell Press Limited, 59A, High Street, Clophill,
Bedfordshire MK45 4BE
Printed by The Lavenham Press

Title page. 6945 GLASFRYN HALL approaches Upwey Junction with the 16.10 Weymouth to Paddington on 31 May 1950. J.C. Flemons, transporttreasury.co.uk

Derek Phillips

The author, now a retired Civil Servant, worked at Yeovil Town Motive Power Depot between 1958 and 1964. Starting as a 16 year old engine cleaner he moved on to become a passed cleaner and latterly a locomotive fireman on freight and local passenger trains between Yeovil, Salisbury and Exeter Central. He worked on most types of Southern Region engines, including the Bulleid Pacifics, King Arthurs, S15 4-6-0s, U and N Moguls and BR Standard classes.

When the ex-GWR engine shed at Yeovil Pen Mill closed in 1959 the locomotives and men were transferred to Yeovil Town, expanding the daily work there. This included evening freight trains to Westbury, passenger services on the branch line to Taunton and also supplying banking engines between Yeovil Pen Mill and Evershot on the Weymouth main line. There was also night banking at Castle Cary, assisting trains to Brewham and Witham, shunting at Hendford Goods and Yeovil to Weymouth excursion trains during the summer. This made for a great variety of interesting work for the drivers and firemen at this busy little shed.

Contents

End of the morning rush hour at Paddington Platform 2 for '61' prairie tank 6103. B.W.L. Brooksbank, Initial Photographics.

4

Introduction

My very first visit to Paddington station occurred in 1951 as a schoolboy of nine years of age; hundreds of similarly aged children gathered together at Frome station from many schools in the area for a visit to the Festival of Britain. The platform was crowded with excited children, the many voices echoing underneath the vast overall station roof as we awaited the train that would take us to London. With a mighty roar and a hissing of steam a gleaming locomotive with a copper capped chimney arrived; there was just a glimpse of a roaring fire and the figures of the driver and fireman before the long train of carriages came to a halt with a squealing of brakes. This was the first journey that I had ever made without one or both of my parents and it was the same for the other children no doubt. We were shepherded aboard by our teachers and within a short space of time the train was on the move complete with a blast on the whistle from the locomotive. I recall that it was a very hot day as we wandered about in organised groups at the Festival of Britain and can also remember that it was a vast exhibition site, too much for a young boy to take it all in, but looking back it was a wonderful day with memories that have lasted ever since, of the Skylon and many other wonders. The journey home by contrast seemed to take forever, a long tiring day combined with wandering about in the hot sunshine, plus gorging myself on a large bag of cherries, leaves me with the memory of being violently ill in the carriage lavatory, and I was only too pleased when the train eventually arrived at Frome where my mother and brother were waiting – happy days.

This book depicts steam locomotives at work on the route between Paddington and Weymouth as it used to be in the age of steam before the advent of mass closures of branch lines and stations and before dieselisation. Paddington, like all other major rail termini in the age of steam was the centre of a perfectly formulated operation as trains arrived, passengers disembarked and the empty coaching stock pulled away by fussy tank engines to the carriage sidings. Departure of the empty stock was usually assisted by the train engine doing its bit to push it out tender first. This engine, a Hall, Castle or King in gleaming green and copper, would halt at the platform end to await clearance for the engine yard at Ranelagh Bridge, just outside the station. Here it would be turned and watered, or if it required coaling it would run out light or on the back of the empty stock (to save a path) to be detached in the carriage sidings close by the great engine sheds at Old Oak Common. Likewise in the incoming direction, tank engines would arrive with empty stock, locomotives would rumble in fresh from turning and oiling and then pull away to destinations far and wide on the Western Region.

The terminus stations of today compared to bygone years seem clinical and efficient despite being plagued by fast-food odours; trains are formed mainly of multiple units arriving and switching off, standing alongside their allotted platform before departing after what seems like only minutes on the return journey. During the 1950s a holiday journey by train was a far different affair, something of an adventure and often in tired, old, faintly mildewy, spare stock far removed from the air-conditioned sanitised trains of today. Hordes of passengers would queue at Paddington with excited children and battered suitcases in readiness to board the train for Weymouth and an annual week away – and they were the better-off ones. The train would be boarded in orderly fashion and tired carriage compartments come alive to voices; dad

7007 GREAT WESTERN backs out of Paddington for turning at Ranelagh Bridge loco yard after arriving earlier from Worcester with the Cathedrals Express, on 1 July 1962. Introduced by the Western Region in 1957, the train ran between Paddington, Oxford, Worcester and Hereford, the locomotives carrying the distinctive and unique blue curved headboard surmounted by a Bishops Mitre with lettering in Gothic style. Emerging as OGMORE CASTLE in July 1946, 7007 was the last express passenger engine built by the GWR at Swindon Works. It was renamed in January 1948 to commemorate the Company, bearing the name of the original GREAT WESTERN of 1846. Nigel Kendall/Railway Images.com.

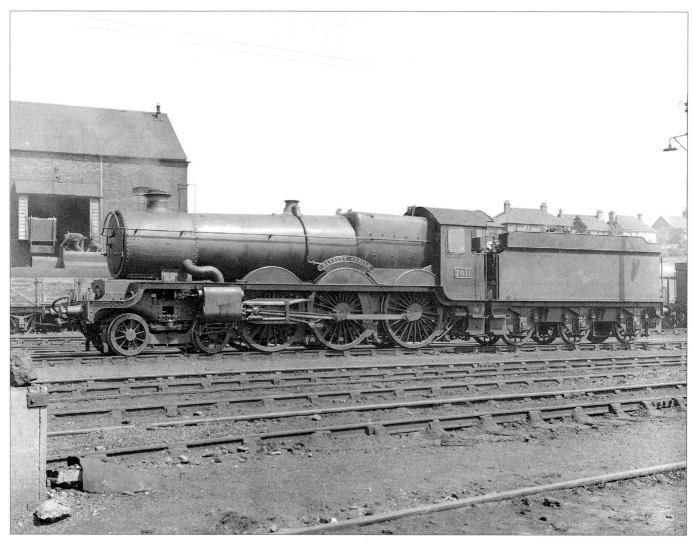

would heave the cases up into the luggage racks and everyone would settle down into their seats. Like as not dad would have had a look at the engine, let alone the kids.

The train is now full and awaiting the time to depart, a glance to the rear and the guard is ready with his green flag and whistle in hand, the magnificent green locomotive and her crew at the front of the train are all ready to go with steam issuing from the safety valves and the roar of the vacuum brake sounding from the chimney. The shrill blast from the guards whistle echoes along the platform complete with a brisk flourish of the green flag and the long train now moves forward slowly at first then gathering speed to faraway Dorset. Out of Paddington amid the hustle and bustle of trains arriving and departing, along through the suburbs the train now moves faster, the wheels clicking and rumbling over the points and crossings.

At Reading the train turns west and heads down the West of England main line, the scenery turning more rural with each passing mile – we still had haystacks then! More excitement as the train enters Wiltshire and the famous white horse carved into the chalk hillside near Westbury comes into view, then across the border and into Somerset, its name derived from the old English *Sumorsaete* 'the land of Summer' and once part of the Anglo Saxon Kingdom of Wessex.

The grime and bustle of London is now far behind as the train travels ever westward, and this is in the days of proper carriages with windows in the doors that passengers could open with long leather straps and lean out for some fresh air amongst the smoke and smuts from the locomotive chimney. As a boy I always managed to get a piece of coal dust in my eye which my mother had to remove with a corner of her handkerchief.

After passing Dorchester West the train is now on the last few miles of the journey, and passengers who have travelled on the route before are now looking out for the first glimpse of the sea, and approaching Upwey a chorus of shouts are heard throughout the train as the blue water of Weymouth Bay and the imposing bulk of the Isle of Portland are glimpsed through the carriage windows.

With the train now slowing rapidly, parents are gathering their children together and pulling suitcases down; then the arrival itself and carriage doors swing open and crowds of people swarm along the platform. Inexplicably, many hardly glance at the travel stained locomotive which has brought them safely from London, and who can blame them as they head for the station exit to enjoy their hols; with fish and chips, buckets and spades, a lovely sandy beach, Punch & Judy, and perhaps a ride on a donkey, maybe even some sunshine. Accommodation typically would be a Saturday-Saturday bed and breakfast hotel under the eagle eye of a ferocious landlady or perhaps a caravan at Bowleaze Cove; the English seaside holiday of the 1950s. Like the Curate's Egg; good in parts.

I would like to thank everybody who has helped me in the preparation of this book and my appreciation is owed to: Weymouth & Portland Borough Council, Network Rail Infrastructures Ltd, Colin Caddy, John Chalraft Rail Photoprints, David Lythgoe, Ben Brooksbank, Yeovil Railway Centre, Dorset History Centre, Bill Waters, The Transport Treasury, Roger Carpenter, John Day, S.V.Blencoe, Bluebell Railway Museum, Stephenson Locomotive Society, Adrian Vaughan, Mike Morant, Kidderminster Railway Museum, John Bird Southern Images, Brian Jackson, Colour Rail. Mr R.E.Toop kindly sent me his photographs some time ago for inclusion and with much sadness I have to report that Mr Toop has since passed away, his photographs of Fairwood Junction and Newbury are included as a tribute to his memory.

7011 BANBURY CASTLE at Weymouth shed after arrival from London. A.E. West, courtesy Mike King.

The beach is already packed at 11.30am on a perfect summer day in the 1950s; the traditional 'meet you by the clock' has been employed by countless visitors and day trippers, for donkeys years now. The clock tower, resplendent in red and blue, was built in 1887 to commemorate the Golden Jubilee of the reign of H.M. Queen Victoria and is a local landmark appearing in many photographs of the town. Note the sparse road traffic compared to today; in the 1950s the majority of holiday makers travelled to the resort by train and motor coach. Graham Herbert courtesy the Dorset History Centre.

Weymouth station and its acres of sidings stretching as far as the eye can see, so different from the scene today. Steam is issuing from a pannier tank shunting a rake of carriages in the middle sidings between the platforms. This view was taken after the removal of the overall roof in 1951 and before the new platforms and signal box of 1957. The white concrete of the new platforms 5 and 6 under construction is prominent on the right. Prior to this, the platforms as viewed from this angle were numbered 1-5 from right to left; from 1957 the order was reversed with platform numbers 1-6 running from left to right. The old station was demolished in 1986 and replaced by a more modern version using the two excursion platforms from the 1957 alterations on the right, plus one short new platform, giving a total of three instead of the previous six. The large goods shed on the left has plenty of wagons waiting loading or unloading, and more carriages are stabled over on the left. Graham Herbert, courtesy Dorset History Centre.

The romance of the big terminus at night. 7029 CLUN CASTLE rests after bringing in a train to Paddington on 3 June 1961. Peter Coster.

8

Chapter 1
Paddington to Reading

The route is as it was during the post-war steam era, when I knew it; train services quoted are from the Western Region Working Timetable for summer Saturdays 1957. I have not related the route to present day operations, but have tried to show it as it was back then, now some half a century ago. Paddington station during the 1950s had a total of sixteen platforms and was divided into two parts – twelve platforms were used for main line trains and the remainder for suburban services. The main station was divided into arrival and departure sections each operated by its own signal box; platforms 1-4 served solely for departures, 5 and 6 could be used for arrivals and departures, 7-11 for arrivals only while 12 was a short parcels platform leading off No.11. The remaining four platforms were used by the Western Region suburban trains with the London Transport Hammersmith line trains using the outer platforms Nos.13 and 16, sharing one pair of tracks with the steam suburban services as far as Royal Oak.

Main line services between Paddington and Weymouth, including the boat trains, were immensely popular with the travelling public in the post-war period and well into the 1950s. Yet this was to be the swansong of the route as it only briefly matched pre-war passenger levels; the end of petrol rationing in the spring of 1950 plus the gradual advent of mass car ownership from the late 1950s and early 1960s, and the emergence of cheap overseas holidays was to bring a major decline in rail passenger travel.

The Channel Islands boat trains had priority over other traffic on the line, in order to connect with the timed sailing from Weymouth Quay. They were the only trains on the route on summer Saturdays to carry the large metal reporting numbers on the locomotive smokebox door. Trains on the route were designated in the Working Timetable as either Weymouth Town or Weymouth Quay, or both, in the case of trains conveying through coaches for the Quay station.

From May until September in the 1950s on Saturdays the first part of the Channel Islands Boat train departed from Paddington at 08.20 followed by the second portion at 08.30, both connecting with the 13.00 sailing to Jersey from Weymouth Quay. The advance relief (08.20) was advertised as running non-stop to Weymouth, whereas the main train (08.30) was booked to pick up passengers only at Reading. The fare in 1953 for a 1st class return from Paddington to Weymouth was 68 shillings (£3.40p); the third class return would cost 45 shillings and 4 pence (£2.27p).

The Cornish Riviera Express (except Saturdays) and the 15.30 Paddington to Penzance conveyed coaches for Weymouth which were slipped at Heywood Road Junction near Westbury. Other services included the 12.30 Paddington to Weymouth worked usually by a Westbury 4-6-0 and crew; a top link turn for Westbury shed (the crew had arrived earlier with the 08.15 semi-fast from Frome) the locomotive worked throughout to Weymouth and returned as far as Westbury with the 18.35 Weymouth-Kensington milk train. The 18.00 to Weymouth would run if required in two or more portions; this train also conveyed a restaurant car which had arrived earlier in the day at Paddington attached to the 09.00 from Weymouth. The main train was usually hauled by an Old Oak Castle as far as Westbury where a Hall would take the train onwards to Weymouth. A late night boat train departed from Paddington at 21.00 for Weymouth Quay in order to connect with the night sailing to the Channel Islands.

5014 GOODRICH CASTLE after arrival at Paddington, alongside platform 8 on 6 July 1963; tail lamp in position ready to run out tender first for turning. www.railphotoprints.co.uk

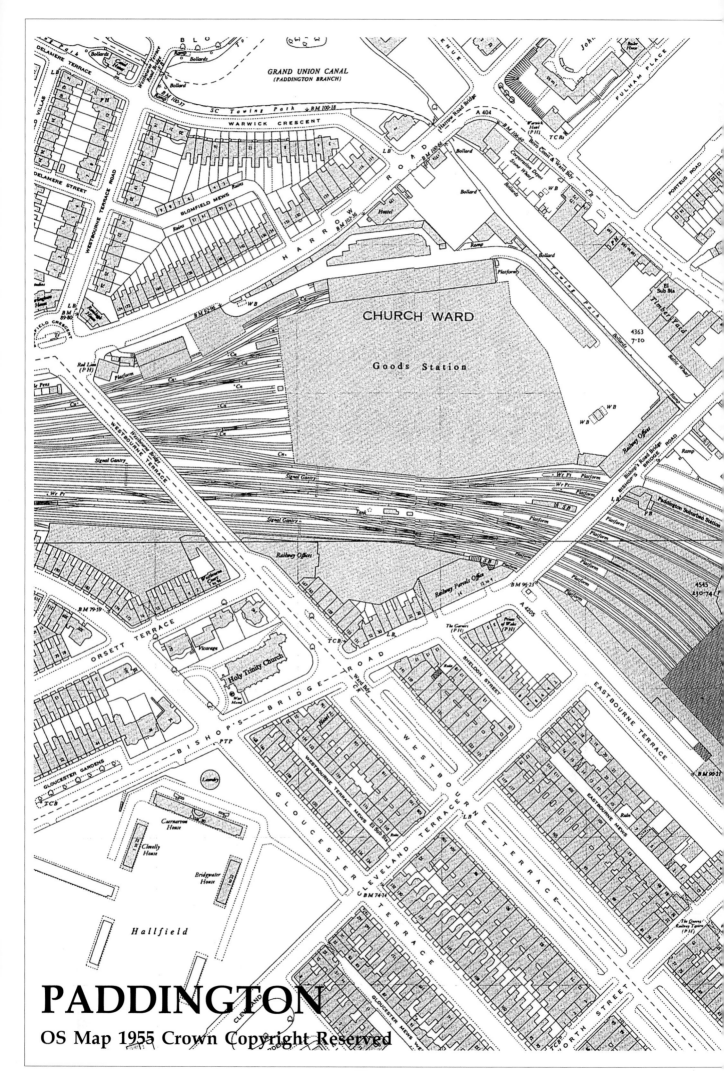

PADDINGTON
OS Map 1955 Crown Copyright Reserved

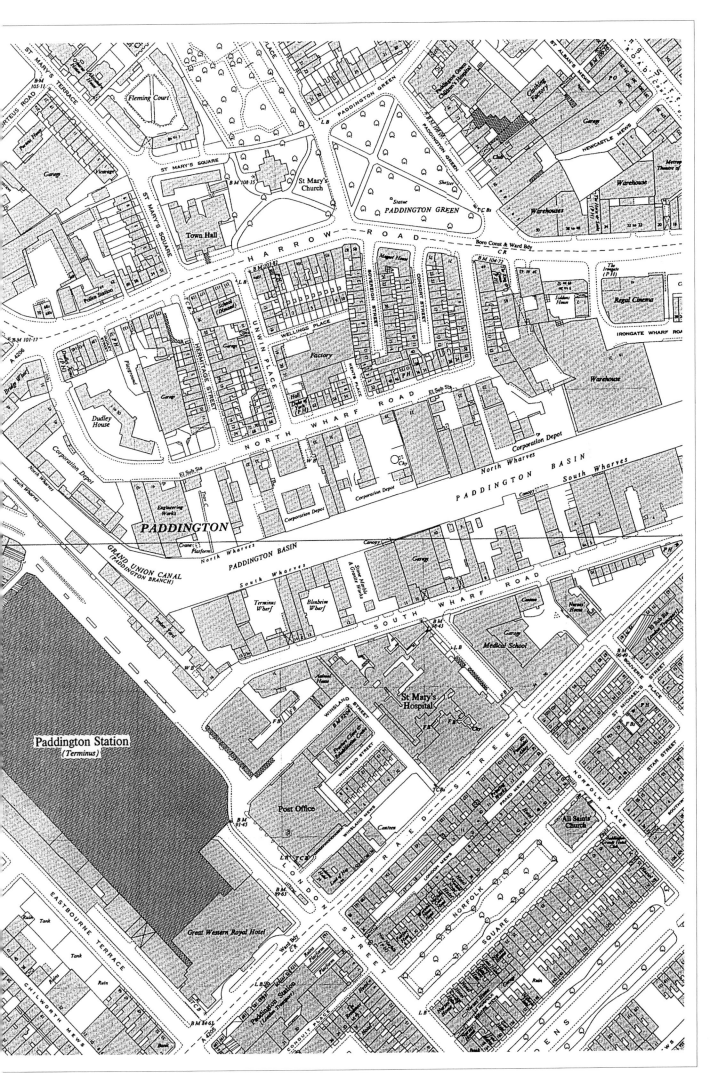

Locomotives travelling to Paddington from Old Oak Common shed were often diagrammed to bring a train of ECS for a preceding service. 6000 KING GEORGE V has arrived with such a train of empty stock on 9 July 1958. J.Harrold, transporttreasury.co.uk

5093 UPTON CASTLE prior to departure with a service to Worcester Shrub Hill from Paddington in February 1963. The ABC Railway Guide for April 1953 informs us that the cost of a first class return ticket is 53 shillings travelling via Oxford, Handborough and Honeybourne. www.railphotoprints.co.uk

6002 KING WILLIAM IV with the Royal Duchy 13.30 Paddington-Penzance at Platform 3 alongside 1004 COUNTY OF SOMERSET.
James Harrold, transporttreasury.co.uk

7914 LLEWENI HALL arrives at Paddington on the last few yards of its journey with a stopping service from Reading in March 1957.
James Harrold, transporttreasury.co.uk

After arriving with the Red Dragon on 13 March 1957, Cardiff Canton Britannia 70028 ROYAL STAR has reversed along the platform and now awaits signal clearance to leave the terminus for turning and engine requirements. The Red Dragon was a weekday service departing Carmarthen at 07.20 (Cardiff 10.00) arriving at Paddington at 12.55 (13.00 SO). The return service departed from Paddington at 17.55 with Swindon as the first booked stop. L.Nicholson, transporttreasury.co.uk

5063 EARL BALDWIN in GWR livery awaits departure from Paddington. The locomotive, dating from 1936, carries the name originally allotted to a 3200 class 4-4-0. Mike Morant Collection.

Veteran record breaking 4-4-0 3440 CITY OF TRURO stands alongside Platform 2 having arrived with empty stock on 23 July 1958. After years as a static display it was restored to full working order January 1957 and allocated to Didcot working ordinary service trains on the DN&S line to Southampton, when not engaged on specials. B.W.L. Brooksbank, Initial Photographics.

94XX pannier 8436 has arrived at the terminus with the empty stock for the next express departing from Platform 4 on 28 June 1962. Passengers walk past the piles of mailbags waiting to be loaded and the doors are open on the coach next to the locomotive, with a loaded trolley at the ready. Note the target No.2 on the bufferbeam; for the benefit of signalmen the carriage pilots were allotted numbers for each turn of duty. B.W.L. Brooksbank, Initial Photographics.

The major main line terminus stations such as Paddington in the 21st Century are worlds away now from the steam age with its constant bustle of trains arriving and departing. Smoke hung in the air and above all was the noise as locos pushed out a train.

Trains would depart for Devon and Cornwall formed of 12 or 14 coaches such was the demand for seats. The last Saturday of July was always the busiest, with nine express services booked to depart for the West of England between 09.30 and 11.05 (in order) to Newquay, Minehead, Paignton, Kingswear, St Ives, Penzance, Paignton, Penzance (2). King and Castle 4-6-0s (in the main) carried the distinctive and well known headboards: *Torbay Express*, *The Royal Duchy*, *The Mayflower*, *Cornish Riviera Express*, to mention a few, standing impatiently at the head of their respective trains with driver and fireman ready for the off, Welsh coal swelling and burning bright in the firebox, the steam pressure gauge needle pointing towards the red line at maximum pressure. Point to point running times were very keen; a non-stop service from Paddington to Reading for instance was booked at 41 minutes, a non-stop run to Newbury at 63 minutes; not

much time to hang about, as there were always speed restrictions both permanent and temporary to be adhered to. To hinder the running further there would be the inevitable signal checks as trains got behind in the crowded schedule.

At the London end, most of the stock for long distance trains was serviced and prepared in the carriage sidings at Old Oak Common. Rakes of empty carriages gained the departure side of Paddington via the up carriage line which crossed the main lines by a flyover (which carried up and down lines and was also used by locomotives travelling to and from Old Oak Common shed) near Old Oak Common East signalbox and then ran by the south side of the down main line. There were two up carriage sidings between Paddington and Subway Junction with the down main line in the middle. Empty stock trains travelling from Paddington to Old Oak Common used the down carriage line on the up side of the layout. At busy times if the down carriage line was blocked, the empty stock would then run to Old Oak Common via the down main line and the flyover.

West London carriage sidings, alongside the down main line near Old Oak Common, stabled the stock for short

distance rush hour services and suburban stock was stabled mainly in Paddington Yard.

Freight traffic was dealt with at Paddington Goods, on the up side just west of the station, with most of the fast night services emanating there. Many long distance freight trains started or terminated at the yards at Old Oak Common. Parcels trains departed from the lengthy platform which extended west from Platform 1 at Paddington. Ranelagh Bridge engine yard on the down side by Royal Oak station had a 65ft turntable and water supply; locomotives not requiring coal were dealt with here instead of travelling to Old Oak Common. The down pilot, often a Castle, sat here awaiting the call and several locomotives could be accommodated at any one time. As many as 80 would be serviced over 24 hours.

The first 36 miles out of Paddington to Reading through the Thames Valley are fairly level on Brunel's classic main line, with a slight rise to Southall easing down to a level route through Slough. The main line as far as Slough in the 1950s was under the control of colour light signalling introduced by the GWR in the 1930s and except for the section between Acton and

The Period between the ending of the Second World War in 1945 and the mid-1950s, before the advent of mass car ownership and cheap overseas holidays, saw a resurgence in rail passenger travel almost, but not quite, equalling pre-war levels. Looking towards the buffer stops from the footbridge on 25 July 1953 reveals a mass of people on platforms 1 and 2 awaiting their respective trains at Paddington. The clock on the far right says 11.35; the stock for the 12.30 to Weymouth was booked off Old Oak Common carriage sidings at 11.30 and will soon arrive at platform 2 on the left. Everyone is smartly attired, men with suits and ties or casual jacket and flannels, with the ladies in frocks and hats. Not a pair of shorts, trainers, jeans or tee shirt in sight. B.W.L. Brooksbank, Initial Photographics.

5001 LLANDOVERY CASTLE departs from Platform 4 with the 18.00 express to Weymouth on 23 May 1958 whilst 7927 WILLINGTON HALL backs down on to a train at Platform 3. The empty stock of another train is running into Platform 5. There is an interesting footnote to the Hall. It languished in Barry scrapyard for years after its withdrawal in December 1965 and its frames live on in the new 1014 COUNTY OF GLAMORGAN now under construction by the GWS at Didcot; the boiler has been restored too, for the new 6880 BETTON GRANGE at Llangollen. B.W.L. Brooksbank, Initial Photographics.

In at 11.20 if running to time 4084 ABERYSTWYTH CASTLE arrives at Paddington with the 08.20 from Weston-Super-Mare on 25 July 1953. There will be a restaurant car on the train and the fare for the journey was 60 shillings for a first class return ticket. Built in May 1925 and allocated new to Plymouth Laira, 4084 was a Bristol Bath Road resident by this time. B.W.L. Brooksbank, Initial Photographics.

57XX 0-6-0PT 9702 on empty stock working at Paddington. The locomotive is specially adapted with condensing apparatus for working freight trains through the Metropolitan tunnels to Smithfield depot. All eleven locos, 9700-9710, were based at Old Oak Common from 1933 until 1962. Mike Morant Collection.

Diesel railcar W17 was especially built for express parcels service in 1936; there was no passenger accommodation and despite its unkempt appearance the railcar is still in GWR brown and cream livery at Paddington in April 1952. Parcel railcars W17 and W34 (dating from 1941) were allocated to Southall shed. G.W.Morant, Mike Morant Collection.

6005 KING GEORGE II departs from Paddington with the 18.10 to Wolverhampton on 27 August 1955. R.C.Riley, transporttreasury.co.uk

6822 MANTON GRANGE departs from Paddington on 18 May 1956 with the first part of the 18.00 to Weymouth. First booked stop is Newbury, at a point to point timing of 63 minutes. The train is conveying a restaurant car that had arrived on the 09.00 from Weymouth earlier in the day. R.C.Riley, transporttreasury.co.uk

9405 at Paddington on 1 September 1962, carrying a peculiar daubing of paint, or some nameless deposit from a shed roof. The empty stock work between Old Oak Common carriage sidings and Paddington station was one of the principal jobs associated with this class.

RANELAGH BRIDGE

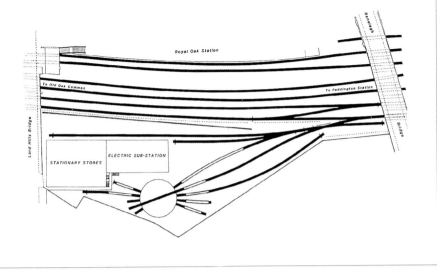

Hayes and Harlington which was equipped with multiple-aspect signals in 1953 and 1955 all signals west of Hayes remained lower quadrant. Quadruple tracks from Paddington as far as Reading and beyond on the Bristol line in the 1950s were designated as down main, up main, down relief, up relief.

Trains departing from Paddington soon pass Royal Oak station, Subway Junction and Westbourne Park. Locomotives would now be getting into their stride as they passed the 91 lever Portobello Junction signalbox, then past Ladbroke Grove signalbox and the giant gas holders of Kensal Green Gas Works. After the gasworks the line now passed underneath the flyover bridge used for empty stock and light engine movements between Old

Left. 7904 FOUNTAINS HALL heads the Royal Duchy away from Paddington along the down main line on 12 March 1958. Formed with chocolate and cream coaches the 13.30 Paddington to Penzance and the reverse 11.00 working from Penzance became the Royal Duchy from 28 January 1957 with 6000 KING GEORGE V in charge of the inaugural down service. R.C.Riley, transporttreasury.co.uk

Below. Ranelagh Bridge engine sidings, just outside Paddington on the down side; it could be glimpsed, tantalisingly, from the platform ends. Those engines from nearer climes, such as Worcester, could return home without coaling and were always dealt with here; there was no coal available at Ranelagh and visiting locomotives ere booked to leave the terminus within an hour or two of arrival. 5045 EARL OF DUDLEY and Britannia 70019 LIGHTNING with Capitals United Express headboard share the place on 12 March 1958. R.C.Riley, transporttreasury.co.uk

Above. 5974 WALLSWORTH HALL with a Paddington-Weymouth express on the down main line at Old Oak Common on 10 September 1955. Distinctive gasholders of Kensal Green Gas Works in the background   R.C.Riley, transporttreasury.co.uk

Left. 6935 BROWSHOLME HALL from Westbury (82D) shed with the 12.30 Paddington-Weymouth on the down main line at Old Oak Common on 10 September 1955. The restaurant car on the train will be detached at Westbury and return to London on the 16.10 from Weymouth. R.C.Riley, transporttreasury.co.uk

Bottom. View east at Old Oak Common East Junction as 4975 UMBERSLADE HALL runs tender-first out of Old Oak shed towards Paddington along the up passenger line on 27 April 1963. It is about to pass under the West London line at Mitre Bridge. B.W.L. Brooksbank, Initial Photographics.

Oak Common and Paddington. West London Junction and the 161 lever Old Oak Common East box controlling the lines in the area of the junction came next, then Old Oak Common West box.

Old Oak Common engine shed, three miles from Paddington on the up side of the line was the largest on the Great Western and probably the largest in the country – certainly it was laid out on a scale lavish beyond that enjoyed by any other railway. The design was attributed to the Chief Mechanical Engineer Churchward; opening on 17 March 1906, it took nearly four years to set out and construct. The main shed included four roundhouse 'units' under one roof, each with an electrically operated 65ft diameter turntable, giving over a hundred locomotive stabling roads. A twelve road lifting and repair shop – 'the factory' –

Top. Saint 4-6-0 2920 SAINT DAVID alongside the coaling stage at Old Oak Common on 2 June 1935. 2920 turned out to be the last Saint in service when withdrawn in October 1953. G.Barlow, transporttreasury.co.uk

Left. A fine looking 8420 at Old Oak alongside the gigantic coal stage on 28 September 1963.

Below. A visitor from Swansea, 7012 BARRY CASTLE of Landore at Old Oak Common on 4 March 1951. Old Oak had plenty of its own of course; of an allocation of nearly 200 locomotives in 1950 some thirty were Castles. R.C.Riley, transporttreasury.co.uk

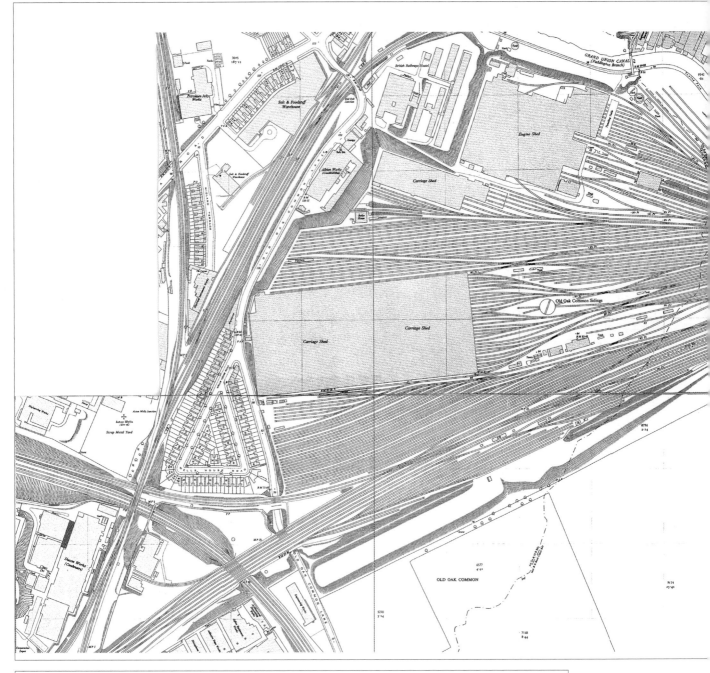

7014 CAERHAYS CASTLE at Old Oak Common. Older Collett tenders increasingly replaced the Hawksworth version in the last years, for the firemen preferred them for their fire iron storage and for their supierior trimming characteristics. J. Davenport, Initial Photographics.

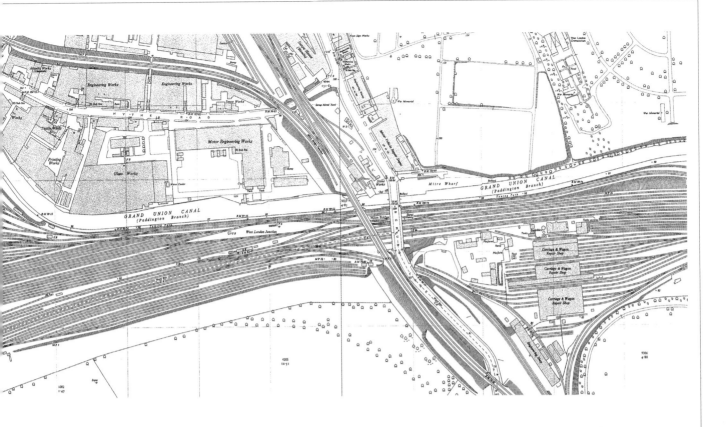

OLD OAK COMMON
OS Map 1955 Crown Copyright Reserved

7036 TAUNTON
CASTLE at Old
Oak Common on
5 June 1960.

General Layout of Old Oak Common 1906

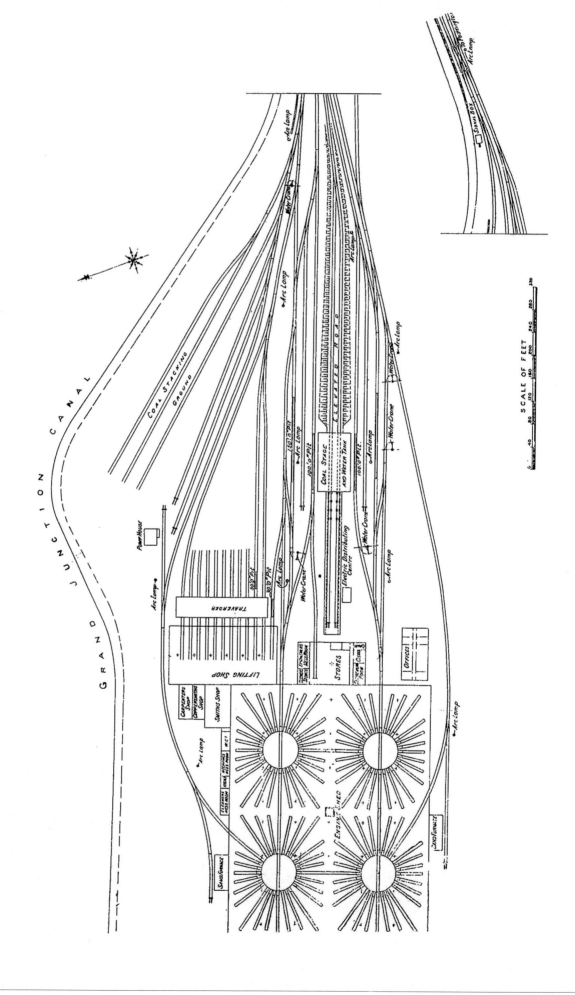

with a 30 ton crane opened at the same time. Locomotives could be lifted for wheels to be taken out and most repairs short of heavy overhauls were possible. The vast two road coal stage established a new standard pattern and was the largest of its type ever built on the GWR. Coal was hand shovelled from wagons into tubs that ran on a steel floor and were tipped, again by hand, over the tender or bunker. Some 500 tons of coal would be shifted in this fashion over a period of 24 hours. The better quality coal was served up from one side, the lesser stuff for goods engines at the other.

Approaching Acton the main line runs alongside the connecting curve, opened by the GWR in 1877, to the North & South Western Junction line at Acton Wells Junction, used chiefly for goods including many inter-regional freight services. Next is Acton station with its four platforms and relief lines and then Acton Yard, one of the most important in the London area;

Top. Laira's 6873 CARADOC GRANGE at Old Oak on 4 March 1951 has been coaled, watered and turned; the tail lamp is in position all ready for the journey tender-first to Paddington. R.C.Riley, transporttreasury.co.uk

Left. A big '61' Prairie and one of Old Oak's own, 6159 at the shed on 8 May 1955. The water tanks above the coal stage contained a combined capacity of 290,000 gallons. G.Barlow, transporttreasury.co.uk

Below. 7018 DRYSLLWYN CASTLE at Old Oak Common shed in August 1962, chalked reporting number 1A52 prominent on the smokebox door. The double chimney was fitted in May 1956. www.railphotoprints.co.uk

81A Old Oak Common
London Division
Shed Code 81A (1949-1965)
Locomotive Allocations 1950
Total locomotives - 193

County 4-6-0
1000/3/8/10/12/15/21/26

Class 15XX 0-6-0PT
1500/1/2/3/4/5.

Class 2251 0-6-0
2276/82

Class 28XX 2-8-0
2826/35/68/95, 3813/52/53

Class ROD 2-8-0
3017

Class 57XX 0-6-0PT
3648/85/88, 3710/54, 4615/44/66/98/99,
5764, 7734/91, 8707/50/51/53/54/56/5759/
60/61/62/63/64/65/67/68/69/70/71/72/73,
9658/59/61, 9700/1/2/3/4/5/6/7/8/9/10/25//
51/54/58/84

Castle 4-6-0
4016/37/75, 5004/14/27/29/35/38/39/40/43/
44/45/55/56/65/66/69/81/85/87, 7001/4/13/
24/25/30/32/33

Class 47XX 2-8-0
4700/1/2/5/7

Hall 4-6-0
4900/23/58/4961/, 5918/31/32/36/37/38/39/
40/41/47/52/62/86/87/96, 6900/10/26/32/44/
53/59/60/62/73/74/83/85/90,7902/3/4/11

King 4-6-0
6001/2/3/7/9/13/14/15/17/18/19/21/28

Class 61XX 2-6-2T
6117/20/21/35/37/41/42/44/49/55/58/59/68

Class 43XX 2-6-0
9302/4/5/6/8/9/15

Class 94XX 0-6-0PT
9401/2/3/4/5/6/18/19/22

Class WD 2-8-0
90101/5.

approximately 28 miles of sidings capable of holding some 2,500 wagons. A vast variety of traffic was handled here including 'local' freight trains to and from depots at Poplar, Victoria & Royal Albert Docks and South Lambeth.

The extensive platform layout at Ealing Broadway enjoyed suburban services as well as Underground Central and District line trains. It was also the starting and terminating point for services to Greenford, worked by 14XX class 0-4-2Ts and auto-trailers, running via West Ealing to Greenford on the GWR Birmingham main line of 1906.

After Hanwell station, trains cross the Brent Valley on the impressive Wharncliffe Viaduct, Brunel's first major structural design and the first contract to be let on the Great Western Railway. The 900ft long viaduct with eight semi-elliptical arches, each spanning 70ft and rising 17ft 6ins, carries trains across the Brent valley at an elevation of 65ft. On the central pier on the south side is a carving of the coat of arms of James Stuart Wortley, Lord Wharncliffe, chairman of the parliamentary committee that steered the passage of the GWR Bill through Parliament. The viaduct became Grade 1 listed on 8 November 1949.

Approaching Southall the engine shed was on the down, left-hand side just east of the station, in the fork of the main line and the freight only branch to Brentford.

Left. Ancient of aspect, double framed/ outside springs 2361 class 0-6-0 2362 in the roundhouse at Old Common on 2 June 1935. It was finally withdrawn from service in November 1946. G.Barlow, transporttreasury.co.uk

Below. 5057 EARL WALDEGRAVE at Old Oak, August 1962.
www.railphotoprints.co.uk

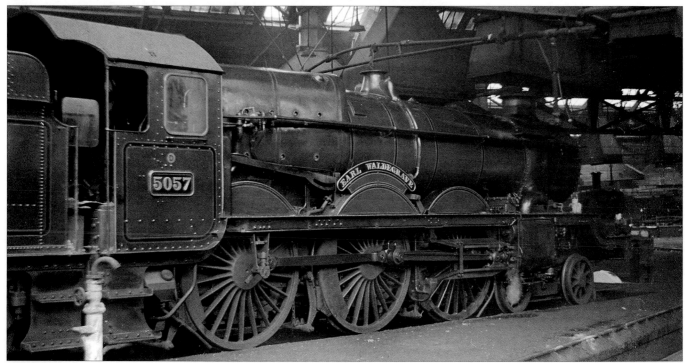

It was especially notable for a large batch of 61XX 2-6-2Ts, which more or less monopolised the commuter work of the London Division.

After the Grand Junction Canal and Hayes and Harlington the station at West Drayton and Yiewsley appeared, the junction for the branches to Staines West and Uxbridge Vine Street. Crossing the river Colne after West Drayton the line now passed through Iver and then Langley, before reaching Slough, junction for the branch to Windsor & Eton. It had an extensive service on weekdays and Sundays with many through trains to Paddington.

Slough engine shed was on the eastern edge of the Windsor branch west of the station. Its main work was the London commuter service (for which had the inevitable 61XX 2-6-2Ts) together with local goods and shunting trips and branch work to Windsor, Aylesbury, Watlington and Marlow.

After passing Burnham and Taplow stations, trains crossed the River Thames on the Maidenhead Bridge, a Brunel masterpiece. The railway is carried across the river on two brick arches which at the time of building were the widest and flattest in the world. Each span is 128 feet with a rise of only 24 feet. Many critics of the day predicted the arches would collapse. The bridge also features in the famous oil painting *Rain, Steam and Speed – The Great Western Railway* by the 19th

6028 KING GEORGE VI stored out of use in the carriage shed at Old Oak Common in August 1962. This was the last year that the Kings reigned supreme on the Western Region of British Railways. 6028 entered service in July 1930 as **KING HENRY II**; it was renamed in January 1937 and withdrawn from service in November 1962. www.railphotoprints.co.uk

1005 COUNTY OF DEVON with an up express at Acton in October 1960. This locomotive was allocated to Bristol Bath Road shed in November 1945 and remained in the Bristol area throughout its working life. When Bristol Bath Road closed to steam in September 1960 to be converted into a diesel depot 1005 was transferred to St Philips Marsh shed and withdrawn on 24 June 1963. A.E.Durrant, Mike Morant Collection.

7331 running well with an up train at Acton under class A headlamps in September 1961. The 43XX class 2-6-0s designed by Churchward were one of the most versatile locomotives ever built by the GWR with a total of 342 constructed between 1911-1932. 7331 entered service in March 1932 as 9309 one of twenty, 9300-9319, differing from the earlier engines by having side window cabs, screw reverse, short safety valve bonnets and outside steam pipes. It had been renumbered 7331 in May 1959. A.E.Durrant, Mike Morant Collection.

5021 WHITTINGTON CASTLE and 1009 COUNTY OF CARMARTHEN with the 10.00 Newquay to Paddington near Acton West Junction on 30 June 1956. They are nearing the end of the 281 mile journey from Cornwall, with a booked arrival time of 16.37 in London. R.C.Riley, transporttreasury.co.uk

Century artist J.M.W. Turner and now exhibited in the National Gallery, London. Maidenhead, nearly 25 miles from Paddington and the junction for the branches to High Wycombe and Bourne End-Marlow.

Twyford was the junction for the branch to Henley on Thames. At times it was an extension of the main line as much as a branch and during the steam era the town's well-heeled commuter clientele enjoyed two daily express trains worked by 4-6-0s direct to Paddington during the morning rush hour with a return service in the evening. After the mile long Sonning Cutting and 36 miles from Paddington, came Reading General. Now

Top. 6870 BODICOTE GRANGE passing Acton West Junction signal box hauling the 14.35 Paddington to Weston-Super-Mare on 30 June 1956; 9704 in the background departs from Acton Yard with a down goods. The 14.35 took a circuitous route travelling down the Berks & Hants to Newbury where the rear portion was detached to form the 16.36 to Westbury via Devizes. The 14.35 ex-Paddington then proceeded to Bristol and Weston-Super-Mare, also via Devizes. R.C.Riley, transporttreasury.co.uk

Middle. The down Torbay Express behind 5079 LYSANDER casts a smoke trail over West Ealing on 11 April 1955. This service was handled in both directions by Castles from Newton Abbot shed. R.C.Riley, transporttreasury.co.uk

Below. 6967 WILLESLEY HALL with an up express at West Ealing on 11 April 1955. R.C.Riley, transporttreasury.co.uk

28XX 2-8-0 2815 approaches Southall on the down relief line with a lengthy freight train on 27 April 1957. A.E.Bennett, transporttreasury.co.uk

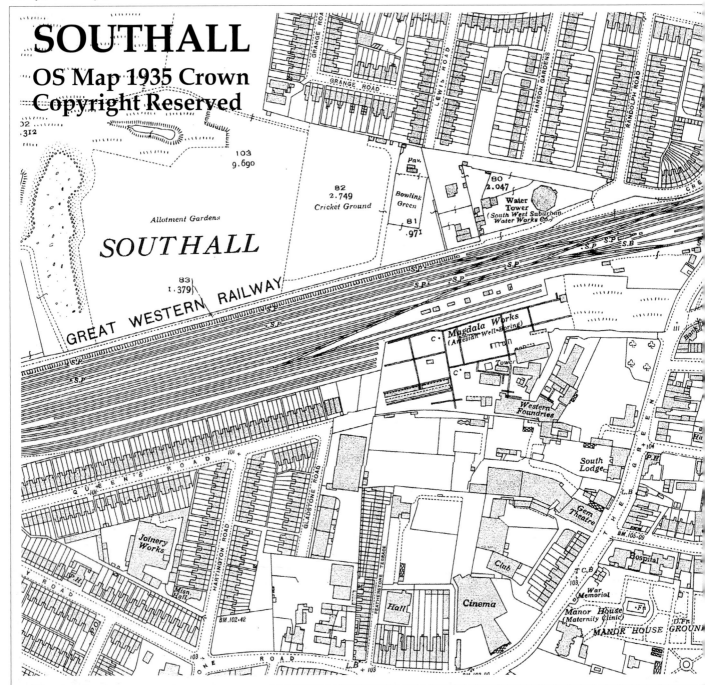

57XX 0-6-0PT 9791 arrives at Southall with a freight off the Brentford branch on 28 October 1961 as Worcester's 7006 **LYDFORD CASTLE** passes on the main line with the 15.10 Paddington to Hereford. B.W.L. Brooksbank, Initial Photographics.

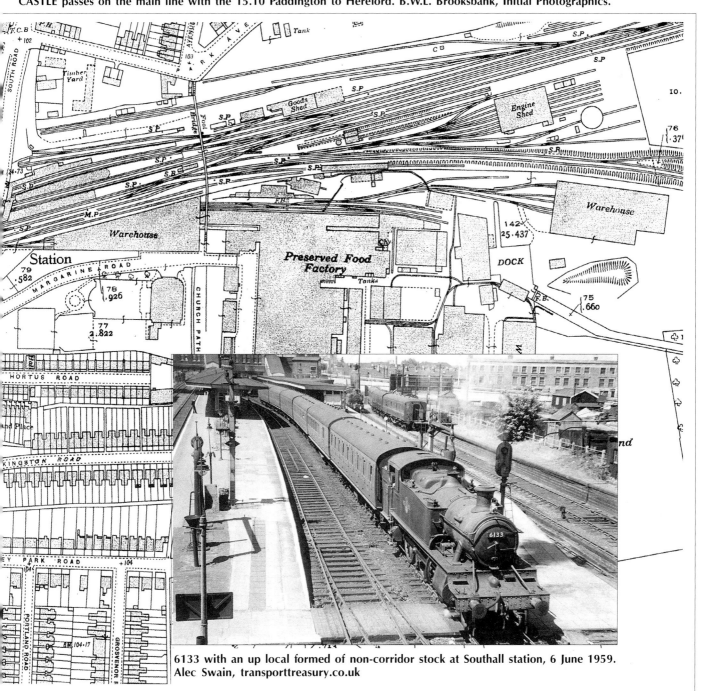

6133 with an up local formed of non-corridor stock at Southall station, 6 June 1959.
Alec Swain, transporttreasury.co.uk

Ex-GWR diesel railcar W13 at Slough on the services to Windsor about 1953. Introduced in 1936 W13 had a seating capacity for 70 passengers and was equipped with twin AEC Ricardo engines. The railcars were very advanced for their day and three are now in preservation. G.W.Morant, Mike Morant Collection.

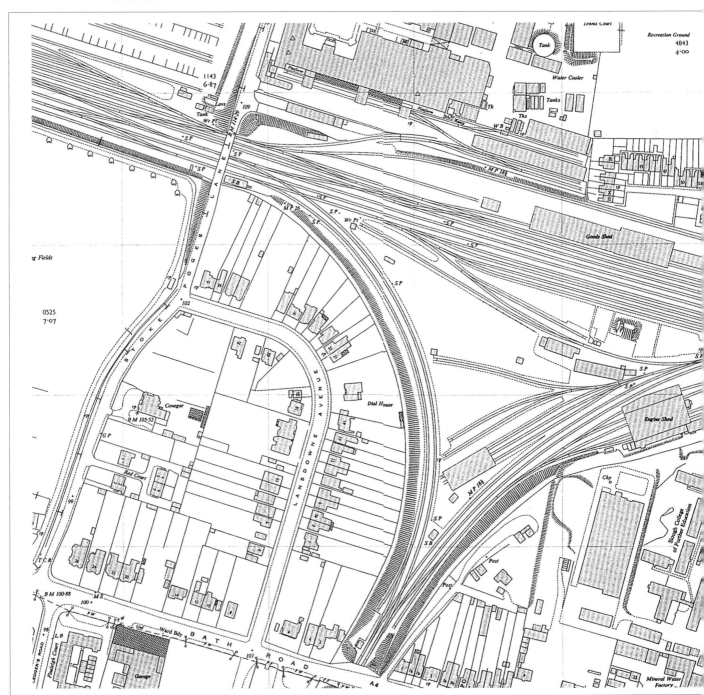

'Big Prairie' 6167 reposes in the yard at Slough on 8 June 1962. The shed supplied engines for local shunting trips and suburban/branch services, on the Windsor, Aylesbury, Watlington and Marlow lines. The 6100 class was built for the accelerated London suburban services out of Paddington and all were allocated new to Old Oak Common, Southall, Slough, Reading and Oxford sheds. By 1962 their thirty-year reign had ended, replaced by DMUs. 6167, built at Swindon in October 1935, was reallocated to Southall in 1964 and withdrawn in 1965. B.W.L. Brooksbank, Initial Photographics.

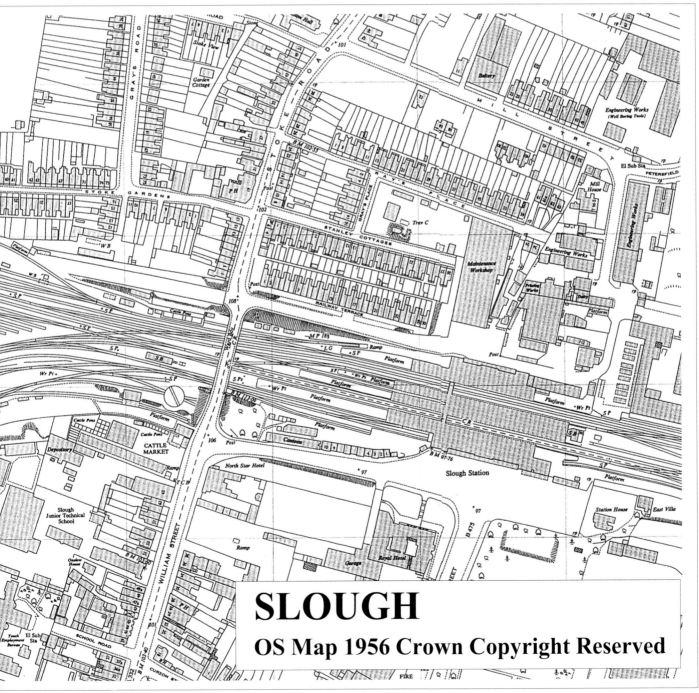

SLOUGH
OS Map 1956 Crown Copyright Reserved

Top. Britannia 70026 POLAR STAR and 6946 HEATHERDEN HALL approach Taplow with the 14.55 Paddington-South Wales express on 25 July 1953. B.W.L. Brooksbank, Initial Photographics.

Middle. The regular Capitals United Express (15.55 Paddington-Fishguard Harbour) ran on 18 April 1957 in two portions, the first departing Paddington at 15.20 behind 70017 ARROW. This is the second portion headed by 70023 VENUS at Ruscombe Siding near Twyford. B.W.L. Brooksbank, Initial Photographics.

Below. 56XX class 0-6-2T 5697 working an up freight train at Sonning Cutting on 19 May 1956. R.C.Riley, transporttreasury.co.uk

6970 WHADDON HALL of Oxford shed backs down towards empty coaching stock at Reading General. A.E.Bennett, transporttreasury.co.uk

7902 EATON MASCOT HALL takes the Bristol main line from Reading General with the 17.05 Paddington to Weston-Super-Mare on 22 April 1956. R.C.Riley,transporttreasury.co.uk

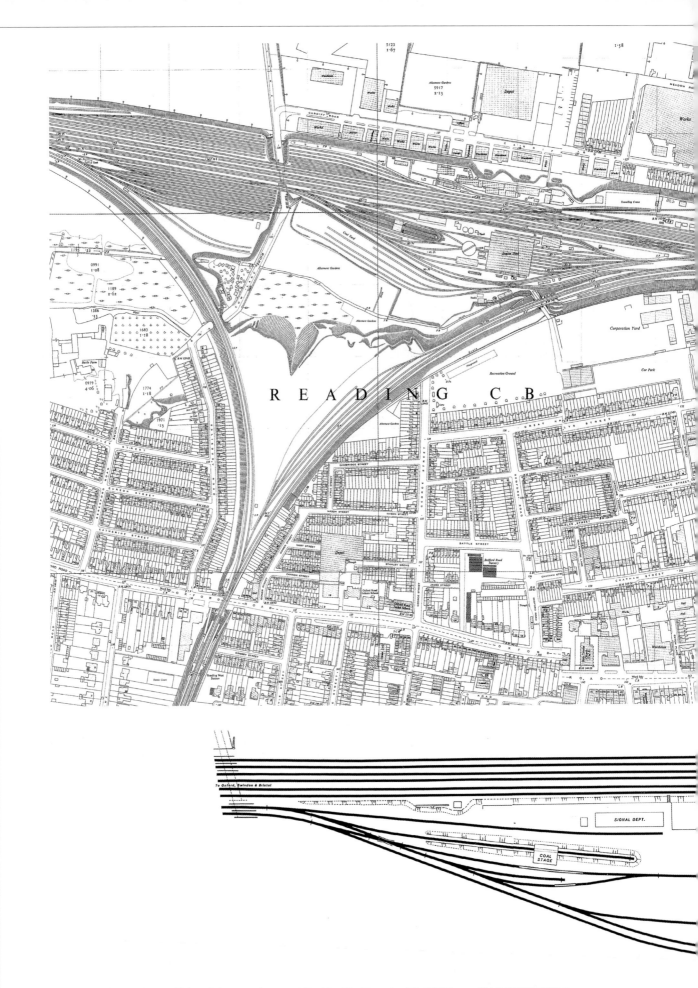

READING STATION AND SHED

OS Map 1961 Crown Copyright Reserved

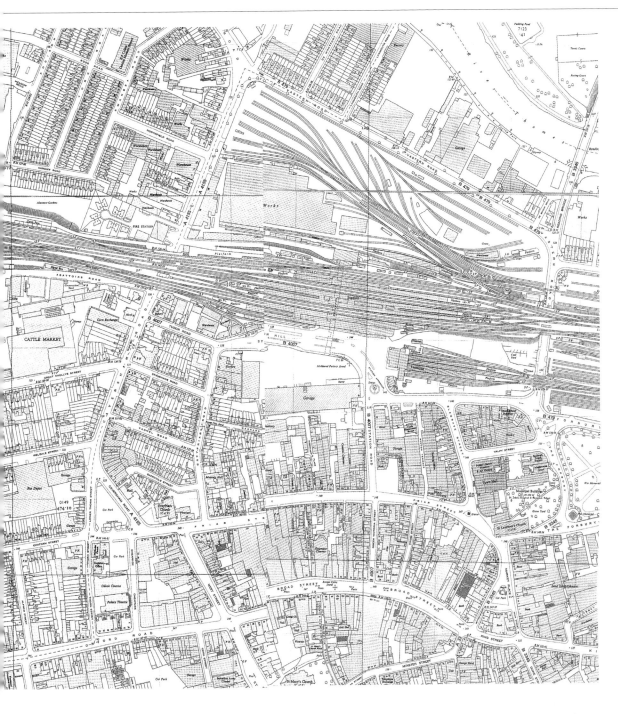

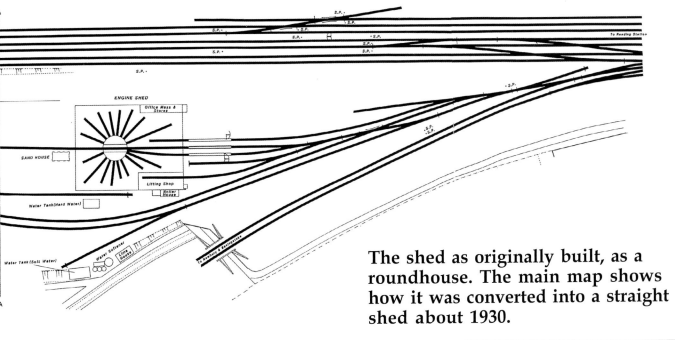

The shed as originally built, as a roundhouse. The main map shows how it was converted into a straight shed about 1930.

81D Reading
London Division
Shed Code 81D (1949-1965)
Locomotive Allocations 1950
Total locomotives - 91

Class MSWJ 2-4-0
1335/36

Class 14XX 0-4-2T
1407/44/47

Class 2251 0-6-0
2208/45/64/99

Class 2301 0-6-0
2573

Class ROD 2-8-0
3025/47

Bulldog 4-4-0
3454

Class 57XX 0-6-0PT
3697, 3715/23/36, 4609/61/65/70, 5762/63/
66/72, 7708/77/88, 9722/49/63/91

Class 28XX 2-8-0
3840/41/45/46

Castle 4-6-0
4085, 5036

Hall 4-6-0
4920/31/39/43/62/89/94/95/98, 5901/33/48/
56/57/59/73/79, 6968/96, 7919

Class 43XX 2-6-0
5375, 6302/12/34/63/66/79/83/93, 7318/20,
9303/7/13/18/19

Class 61XX 2-6-2T
6100/1/3/5/30/45/53/62/63

Grange 4-6-0
6802/64/65

Class 94XX 0-6-0PT
9410/11/12/20/23

being reconstructed from the ground up, during the 1950s it had main and relief platforms serving up and down lines, plus bay platforms including three at the west end for local services. There was a through line for up trains only between the up and down main platform lines; connecting spurs also allowed the transfer of freight and passenger trains to the nearby Southern station at Reading South. Reading engine shed lay west of the station in the triangle of lines formed by

Below. 7017 G. J. CHURCHWARD runs through Reading General on the up through line with an express for Paddington on 7 September 1958. A.E.Bennett, transporttreasury.co.uk

Bottom. 6002 KING WILLIAM IV arrives with the up *Mayflower* (08.30 Plymouth North Road-Paddington) at Reading General on 26 March 1959. B.W.L. Brooksbank, Initial Photographics.

the route from Reading General station to Reading West, the Bristol main line, and the west curve connecting the Bristol main line with Reading West at Oxford Road Junction. It was an old eight-road shed, and highly unusual in that it had been converted from a roundhouse back in the 1930s. Access was gained from either end of the layout; locomotives running in from the west would approach the coal stage and after being serviced would move over the turntable and be stabled in the running shed, locomotives arriving from the station area would run in on the shed bypass line south of the building to gain access to the coaling stage.

Left. A pilot loco was always on stand-by at Reading General. Churchward 43XX 2-6-0 6379 stands in traditional position as the up pilot in No.5 East Bay on 26 July 1962, in readiness to replace an ailing locomotive on a Paddington bound service. B.W.L. Brooksbank, Initial Photographics.

Middle.
Up from its unlikely home, Cardiff East Dock on 8 June 1963; 5081 LOCKHEED HUDSON at Reading shed a few months before withdrawal in October of the same year. 5081 entered service in May 1939 as PENRICE CASTLE and was renamed in January 1941. C.L.Caddy.

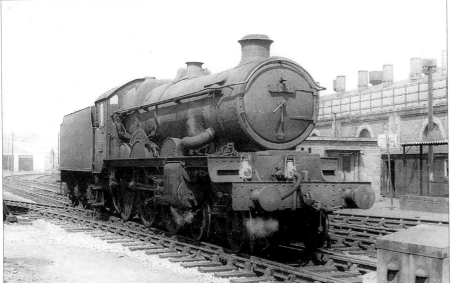

Below. Reading shed in the foreground with 7037 SWINDON running past, approaching the station with an up stopping train on 17 September 1955. This was the last Castle built and was named by HRH Princess Margaret on 15 November 1950 at Swindon Works in honour of the Jubilee of the Borough. A.E. Bennett, transporttreasury.co.uk

Above. Reading West station. Ahead is Oxford Road Junction; the lines to the left lead to the original GWR main line to Bristol at Reading West Junction, the lines to Reading General curve away to the right. R.C.Riley, transporttreasury.co.uk

Left. 6918 SANDON HALL with a down empty stock train passing through Reading West on 30 August 1963. H.F.Wheeler Collection.

Bottom. Westbury's 7924 THORNYCROFT HALL with a down passenger train at Reading West on 21 April 1956. R.C.Riley, transporttreasury.co.uk

Chapter 2
Reading to Westbury

West of Reading trains for Weymouth and the West of England turn south, through Reading West station and, a mile further on, Southcote Junction, where the line to Basingstoke branched off to the left. A 40mph-speed restriction over the junction was in place here for trains using the route to Newbury. The section between Oxford Road Junction and Southcote Junction would be very busy on summer Saturdays not only with the West of England trains, but also with the cross-country services from the Midlands to the Southern Region, plus the regular stopping services between Reading and Basingstoke.

Trains on the West of England route now pass through Calcot and Theale, where water would be taken from the troughs at Aldermaston. Thence through Midgham and Thatcham before passing Newbury Race Course station. On race meetings it was served by many extra trains from all over the Western Region including the well-known 'members specials' from Paddington; two of the Weymouth services, the 12.30 ex-Paddington and the 09.00 from Weymouth made special stops at the Race Course station when racing was on. At Newbury East Junction the DN&SJR line from Didcot converged with the main line. Newbury was the junction for lines to Didcot, Southampton and Lambourn. Down and up West of England main line trains not booked to stop here would take the through lines for which there was a 60mph speed limit. The 18.00 Paddington to Weymouth was booked to

5973 ROLLESTON HALL with an up stopping passenger service near Reading West on 21 April 1956. R.C.Riley, transporttreasury.co.uk

5901 HAZEL HALL with a down passenger train, approaching Southcote Junction on 20 April 1956. R.C.Riley, transporttreasury.co.uk

Top. 6001 KING EDWARD VII with the up Torbay Limited near Theale in May 1935. Dr Ian C. Allen, transporttreasury.co.uk

Left. Bulldog 4-4-0 3444 CORMORANT with a Weymouth to Paddington express near Theale in May 1933. Dr Ian C Allen, transporttreasury.co.uk

Below. 6991 ACTON BURNELL HALL with a down express at Aldermaston on 7 July 1956. The reporting numbers on the smokebox door are formed of 16 inch white figures on a black background, fitted into a slotted frame approximately 3ft long; they were designed to be seen by signalmen at a distance of a quarter of a mile. R.C.Riley, transporttreasury.co.uk

Top. 6010 KING CHARLES I on the turntable at Newbury Racecourse station on 5 March 1960; Newbury Racecourse signal box in the background. R.C.Riley, transporttreasury.co.uk

Left. 4090 DORCHESTER CASTLE runs past Newbury East Junction signal box on 7 July 1956 with the 15.20 (SO) Paddington to Kingswear. The train was booked to call at Dawlish, Newton Abbot, Torre, Torquay, Goodrington Sands Halt, Churston & Kingswear. R.C.Riley, transporttreasury.co.uk

Below. Newbury Middle signal box in the foreground as 4088 DARTMOUTH CASTLE approaches with the down milk empties on 21 April 1956. R.C.Riley, transporttreasury.co.uk

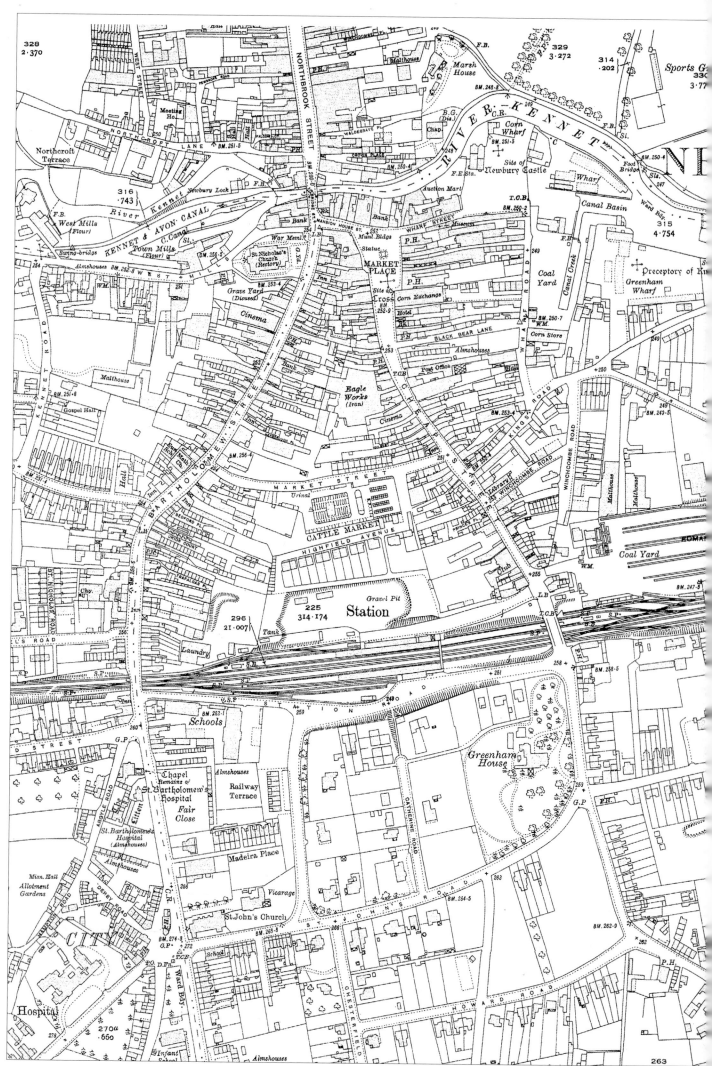

run non-stop to Newbury whereupon the rear four coaches of the eleven coach train were detached to run to Trowbridge via the Devizes line, leaving the main train to travel onwards to Westbury via the direct route. Lambourn branch trains used the bay platform at the west end of the up platform, the single-track line running parallel to the up main line for approximately half a mile before turning northwards towards Lambourn 12½ miles away.

One mile west of the main Newbury station the DN&SJR line to Winchester (Chesil) and Southampton branched off southwards at Enborne Junction and for all down West of England trains from hereon there was an almost unbroken ascent as far as the summit at Savernake. The maximum loading for a King on the route was 500 tons, and for a Castle 455 tons.

Stations at Kintbury, Hungerford and Bedwyn would be passed on the ascent to the summit and at any one of the stations an inevitable signal check due to the slow progress of a train in front would deter fast running services on summer Saturdays. The down WR main line ran underneath the bridge carrying the MSWJR (Midland & South Western Junction) line before running past Wolfhall Junction. Savernake Low Level station had two signal boxes, East and West and a bay platform served the 5¼ mile branch to Marlborough. Up freights requiring assistance would be banked as

far as Savernake Low Level on the ascent from Westbury with the assisting engine allowed 55 minutes to return light engine to Westbury.

From Savernake there is a long descent towards Westbury, always useful to a fireman, especially if a locomotive was not steaming as perfectly as it should, allowing time to rally the steam pressure around. Wootton Rivers Halt with its staggered platforms, Pewsey, Manningford Halt and Woodborough are passed before reaching Patney & Chirton 81 miles from Paddington and junction for the Devizes line. From here the single-track Devizes branch ran alongside the up main line for one mile before branching off. The 09.34 semi-fast Reading General-Weymouth (SO) would travel as far as Patney & Chirton and then follow the circuitous route through Devizes to Westbury. Certain through

Right. **Newbury on 7 July 1956 with 2240 in the foreground which has come up over the DN&S route from Southampton and now stands on the up relief line before departing for Didcot as 6910 GOSSINGTON HALL arrives at the down platform. Signals have also been lowered for a train travelling through the station on the up main. L.Nicholson, transporttreasury.co.uk**

After departing from Westbury and travelling via the Devizes line 4962 RAGLEY HALL calls at Newbury with the 11.48 Westbury to Reading stopper on 5 March 1960. Newbury station was equipped with through and platform lines plus bay platforms for local services on the up side facing east and on the down side facing west. Trains on the Lambourn branch services used a bay platform facing west on the up side of the station. R.C.Riley, transporttreasury.co.uk

0-6-0PT 4665 in the Lambourn branch bay at Newbury about 1958; of as much note as the pristine pannier tank is the Austin lorry in British Railways carmine and cream livery. Mike Morant.

Steam issues from the safety valves of 5906 LAWTON HALL standing alongside the down platform at Newbury on 1 July 1956. Pannier 3723 stands on the up relief line in the background. L. Nicholson, transporttreasury.co.uk

6131 at Newbury with the 13.18 Reading to Westbury via Devizes on 2 September 1961. This train had run non-stop from Reading under class A headlamps, whereupon it will now form an all stations stopper to Westbury. R.E.Toop.

Top. A down express hauled by 5032 USK CASTLE runs through Newbury on 2 September 1961. R.E.Toop.

Left. 6965 THIRLESTAINE HALL approaches Hungerford with the 14.45 Kensington-Plymouth milk empties on 8 July 1956. Some of the tank wagons will be detached at Castle Cary for onward transit to the Weymouth line. R.C.Riley, transporttreasury.co.uk

Bottom. The down inner home signal at Hungerford has halted the progress of 6959 PEATLING HALL, which now restarts its journey hauling the 08.50 Paddington to Paignton on 12 July 1958. 6959 was the first modified Hall. R.C.Riley, transporttreasury.co.uk

Top. 43XX 2-6-0 6306 hauls an up freight near Bedwyn on 8 July 1956. R.C.Riley, transporttreasury.co.uk

Left. 5977 BECKFORD HALL runs past Wolfhall Junction signal box with a Reading-Westbury stopping train on 15 July 1961. J.J Smith Collection, Bluebell Railway Museum.

Bottom. Savernake Low Level with a Marlborough branch train in the bay platform on the left and 5956 HORSLEY HALL heading the 19.05 Newbury to Weymouth on 8 July 1961. J.J Smith, Bluebell Railway Museum.

trains between Paddington and Bristol used the Devizes route including the 14.35 Paddington to Weston-Super-Mare and the 11.22 Bristol Temple Meads to Reading, as well as trains diverted on Sundays by engineering works. Trains would join the Thingley Junction-Bradford Junction route at Holt Junction and at Bradford Junction would either be routed to Trowbridge and Westbury or onto the Avon Valley line travelling to Bathampton Junction and joining the Paddington-Bristol main line.

After Lavington and Edington & Bratton stations came Heywood Road Junction, east of Westbury. Through trains not booked to stop at Westbury station would take the avoiding line, and both the 08.20 and 08.30 Paddington to Weymouth Quay Boat trains were booked to stop at Heywood Road for footplate crew changes. The 08.20 had a booked arrival at 10.18 and away at 10.20 via the avoiding line (this train, with same locomotive, connected with the inward

Top. 6994 BAGGRAVE HALL near Pewsey with the 12.30 Paddington to Weymouth on 9 July 1956. The locomotive will return to Westbury with the 18.35 Weymouth to Kensington milk tanks. R.C.Riley, transporttreasury.co.uk

Right. 28XX 2-8-0 2846 arrives at Westbury from the Trowbridge line with a freight train around 1954. The Berks & Hants line to Newbury and Reading, known as the 'Patney' to local railwaymen, diverges to the right. A.Butler, Kidderminster Railway Museum.

Below. 1011 COUNTY OF CHESTER pulls empty coaching stock from the back road at Westbury in April 1963; the stock will then be reversed into the up platform to form a local stopping service to Swindon. www.railphotoprints.co.uk

Signalled for the Trowbridge line with the distant signal arm for Hawkeridge Junction signal box remaining at caution, 7924 THORNYCROFT HALL and a 2-6-0 head a train of empty coaching stock past Westbury North signal box. A. Butler, Kidderminster Railway Museum.

4014 KNIGHT OF THE BATH runs through Westbury on 7 May 1927 with the second portion of the down Cornish Riviera Express. The two rear coaches destined for Weymouth have been slipped from the train and will enter the station under their own momentum, to be being brought to a halt by the guard operating the brake from his compartment. Kidderminster Railway Museum.

Bulldog class 4-4-0 3367 EVAN LLEWELLYN working a local passenger train at Westbury on 10 May 1932; it was constructed at Swindon in 1903 and withdrawn from service in September 1935. The locomotive was named after a GWR Director who had served in the Boer War. Kidderminster Railway Museum.

at 12.32 and due in Weymouth at 15.07. The 15.30 Paddington-Penzance (SX) booked through Heywood Road Junction at 17.11 also slipped a Weymouth portion. It was collected by a pilot at 17.18 with an arrival time into Westbury station at 17.21 and worked forward attached to the rear of the 16.25 Bristol Temple Meads-Weymouth which, if running to time, would be waiting in the station. This train was due off Westbury at 17.27. The slip coach off the 15.30 reached Weymouth in less than 3½ hours at 18.57, which was good going. The 10.30 ex-Paddington ceased slip working at Heywood Road Junction in September 1958 and the 15.30 ex-Paddington slip service was withdrawn from January 1959.

After passing the wartime spur to Hawkeridge Junction, the line into Westbury converged with the original Wilts Somerset & Weymouth line running in from Trowbridge east of the station. Westbury was the hub for Weymouth services from other parts of the country including Bristol Temple Meads, Chippenham, Cardiff,

bound sailing from Jersey and reached Paddington at 19.30).

Hard on the heels of the 08.20 was the 08.25 Paddington-Penzance, which was booked to pass Heywood Road Junction at 10.27 also running via the avoiding line. The 08.30 Paddington-Weymouth Quay had a booked arrival of 10.33 at Heywood Road Junction also to change footplate crews and away at 10.35 also travelling via the avoiding line.

Two down main line services, the *Cornish Riviera Express* and the 15.30 Paddington-Penzance (SX) still slipped coaches for Weymouth at Heywood Road Junction for much of the 1950s, with the main train continuing on the avoiding line. The slipped coaches were collected and taken into Westbury station by a pilot locomotive. The Cornish Riviera Express was booked to slip (except Saturdays) and pass Heywood Road Junction at 12.10; however if the relief (10.35 ex-Paddington) was also running, then the relief would convey the slip instead of the main train. The slipped coaches would be attached to the 11.25 Chippenham-Weymouth booked away from Westbury

6924 GRANTLEY HALL at Westbury after arrival with a train from Reading in May 1963. www.railphotoprints.co.uk

WESTBURY

OS Map 1941 Crown
Copyright reserved

New
Westbury
Iron Works

Westbury
Station

GREAT WESTERN RAILWAY

Brook Mill
Farm

Engine
Shed

STERN RAILWAY

340
·666

341
4·611

342
·160

331
·137

17·535

330
1·727

332
5·103

216

343
8·562

335
14·059

211

333
2·332

327 · 213

204

325
4·485

345

323
·495

199

322
·533

321
1·441

328
11·892

328a

316
4·241

315 1·446

317
2·635

318
22·230

346
2·935

346
4·866

346a
·071

311
4·864

11a
·46

312
4·592

312b
2·381

311b
·139

312a
·138

313
1·615

347
5·803

347
4·552

348
21·363

70
2·558

360
1·450

443
16·890

444
8·230

444a
·253

444a
6·195

444c
2·766

444c

557
·361

344
·934

445
3·891

555
·976

556c
·507

555a
·721

556d
2·746

556b
·279

556a
5·973

562
2·511

559
·465

560
·004

560a
·095

558
·134

342
·542

343
11·082

556
19·113

343

Reservoir

Tank

Tank

Tank

Tank

Sluice

Sluice

Cattle
Pens

Crane

Goods
Shed

S.B.

S.B.

S.B

S.Ps

S.P.

S.P.

S.P.

S.P.

S.P.

S.P.

S.P.

S.P.

S.P.

S.P

S.P

WM

WM

F.P.

F.P.

F.P.

F.P.

F.P.

F.P.

TRAMWAY

231

231

226

223

BM 25

S.B.

56

Activity at Westbury as a passenger train signalled for the Trowbridge line awaits departure with a Salisbury to Bristol cross-country service. Westbury North signal box dating from 1899 when the station was extensively rebuilt originally had an 82-lever frame, uprated to 99 levers in 1949. www.transporttreasury.co.uk

Westbury was always an important rail junction, as demonstrated here with a Portsmouth-Cardiff cross-country service on the left signalled for the Trowbridge line and a perishable freight on the up goods loop alongside a pannier tank on station pilot duties. The 2,478ft up loop installed in 1915 would accommodate several goods trains at the same time during busy periods. The plant yard on the far right belongs to A.J.Farr Ltd, Civil Engineers, becoming part of the Bovis Group in later years.www.transporttreasury.co.uk

Birmingham, Wolverhampton and Weston Super Mare. Trains from Bristol & Cardiff approached Westbury via the Avon Valley route from Bathampton Junction while services from Chippenham, Birmingham and Wolverhampton would arrive via Chippenham, Thingley Junction and the original Wilts Somerset. & Weymouth line.

On summer Saturdays in 1957 passenger trains arriving at and travelling through Westbury for Weymouth (*marks those not stopping) included six services ex-Bristol at 05.45, 08.05, 09.10*, 12.45, 16.25, 17.02 and two trains ex-Birmingham Snow Hill 07.50* and 08.00*. Other Weymouth services included the 11.25 from Chippenham, 09.34 from Reading General (via Devizes), 08.30 from Weston Super Mare, 11.05 from Wolverhampton, and the 12.30, 18.00 and 21.00 from Paddington. Local services starting at Westbury for Weymouth departed at 09.27, 16.15 and 20.50.

Trains arriving at Westbury from Weymouth included the 07.17 to Chippenham, 0815, 12.40, 13.45, 19.30 to Bristol Temple Meads, the 09.00, 11.12 (the 15.45 Weymouth-Paddington ran via the avoiding line) and 16.14 to Paddington, 09.25 and 10.20 to Wolverhampton, 10.00 to Birmingham Moor Street, 13.35 and 16.15 to Cardiff.

Pannier 3746 with a short pick-up goods at Westbury on 25 August 1963. Local freight services included trips to Frome, Trowbridge, Savernake, Warminster, Radstock and Chippenham. S.V.Blencoe.

5967 BICKMARSH HALL arrives at Westbury with an express freight train (authorised to run at the maximum speed of 35 mph) on 27 August 1963. 5967 is now in preservation and undergoing a lengthy restoration on the Northampton & Lamport Railway. S.V. Blencowe.

With Westbury South signal box in the background, Bulleid light Pacific 34048 CREDITON pulls away from the down yard with a freight train for Salisbury in June 1963. The engine shed can be glimpsed on the right. www.railphotoprints.co.uk

Westbury engine shed on 5 May 1963; constructed to the Churchward straight pattern, in brick under a slate roof, the GWR allocation in 1950 was 75 locomotives. Brick built coaling stage with 45,000-gallon water tank forming the roof is to the right. C.L.Caddy.

The 16.15 had through coaches for Birmingham which were detached at Westbury and conveyed onwards to Birmingham as the 18.19 from Westbury. Two services from Weymouth, the 14.32 and 18.10, terminated at Westbury. There was also an empty stock train from Weymouth departing at 11.50; this was the returning stock, which had travelled to Weymouth earlier as the 09.27 from Westbury. The 18.35 Weymouth to Kensington milk train would continue its journey from Westbury via Thingley Junction and Chippenham. The station was also central to the cross-country services from Cardiff and Bristol to Portsmouth via Salisbury, the lines to Salisbury and Frome separating to the south of the station. Banking locomotives assisted trains on the Salisbury line and three signal boxes controlled the station layout: North, Middle and South.

Westbury engine shed opened in 1915, to the south of the station alongside the down goods yard and accessed from a connection near Westbury South signal box. It became the parent depot in 1932 for Frome (6 locos) and Salisbury (7 locos); the allocation in 1950 comprised 75 locomotives including one County, three Stars, sixteen Halls and two Grange 4-6-0s.

Left. 4925 EYNSHAM HALL on the 65ft overgirder turntable at Westbury about 1955. A. Butler, Kidderminster Railway Museum.

Bottom left. 3826 COUNTY OF FLINT at Westbury; with large outside cylinders and short wheelbase, the class were known as 'Churchward's Rough Riders.' 3826 was withdrawn from service in August 1931. Kidderminster Railway Museum/Collection.

Below. 7809 CHILDREY MANOR at Westbury shed on 11 May 1958 with 4500 class 2-6-2T No.5554 just in view behind the tender. 7809, built in April 1938, was amongst the first twenty locomotives of the class to incorporate the wheels and motion from withdrawn 43XX 2-6-0s. W.Potter, Kidderminster Railway Museum/Collection.

5003 LULWORTH CASTLE accelerates along the Westbury avoiding line near Fairwood Junction with a down express on 22 July 1956. R.C.Riley, transporttreasury.co.uk

Approaching the convergence of the Westbury station line with the western end of the avoiding line. 4087 CARDIGAN CASTLE approaches Fairwood Junction from Westbury station on 23 April 1955. Photograph R.E. Toop.

Chapter 3
Westbury to Yeovil

At Fairwood Junction west of Newbury, where the station lines and the western end of the Westbury avoiding lines converge, water troughs were installed just west of Fairwood Junction signal box to serve the up and down main lines. Two water tanks alongside the down main line fed the troughs, replenishing them within three minutes after the passage of a locomotive picking up water. From here there is a 1½ mile ascent to Clink Road Junction signal box which controlled the junction with the eastern end of the Frome avoiding line and the original Wilts, Somerset & Weymouth line into Frome station with its beautiful Grade II listed Brunel overall roof of 1850, designed by J.R.Hannaford, Brunel's senior assistant. As well as being served by Weymouth line trains, the station was also the junction for Radstock and Bristol via the North Somerset line, served by a bay adjacent to the up platform, or from the up platform if the train was arriving via the East Somerset line from Wells and Witham.

The 15.40 Weymouth to Paddington was not booked to stop at Westbury and called instead at Frome with a booked arrival at 17.27; passengers and mail

from Jersey & Guernsey travelling to Bristol disembarked and resumed their journey via the North Somerset line on the 17.55 Frome-Bristol which was normally formed of seven coaches, running under Class A headlamps stopping only at Radstock West and Pensford.

Frome and Bristol footplate crews would work the North and East Somerset branch lines on a circular journey; one of the regular workings was the 15.30 (SO) Frome to Yatton which after picking up passengers from the 12.30 Paddington-Weymouth (due 14.57 SO) would travel to Witham, then to Wells via the East Somerset branch and onwards to Yatton. After arrival at Bristol Temple Meads it would then form the 17.20 to Frome via Radstock with a booked arrival at Frome of 18.30. The little wooden Frome engine shed, with its single road on the up side behind the goods shed became an outstation of Westbury in 1932. There was not much room and locomotives were also stabled on the nearby sidings serving Bailey's malthouse, much to the annoyance at times of the shunters, who had to move often dead locomotives out of the way. The allocation of approximately ten pannier tanks was

employed on local services including the North Somerset and East Somerset lines and shunting duties.

Trains departing Frome gained access to the down West of England main line just over a mile away at Blatchbridge Junction where the 28 lever frame signal box controlled the junction of the western end of the Frome avoiding line and the lines into Frome station. Witham station, five miles south-west of Frome, was the junction of the East Somerset line to Wells and Yatton. A unique feature was the small wooden overall roof train shed over the bay platform for branch trains which only covered one carriage. Services on the branch consisted of a total of four weekday trains plus one freight.

Brewham signal alongside the down main line stood at the top of the gruelling ascent eastward from Castle Cary and a short siding was provided by the up main line for banking locomotives awaiting a path back down to Castle Cary. When I was a fireman at Yeovil Town we used to work the night banker, usually a prairie or pannier tank, assisting freight trains from Castle Cary to Brewham. A timing of fourteen minutes was allowed for engines returning light engine to Castle Cary and if Brewham signal box was

5925 EASTCOTE HALL, paired with a Collett 3500 gallon tender, diverges onto the Westbury station line with an up express at Fairwood Junction on 2 July 1955. R.E.Toop.

6913 LEVENS HALL takes the Westbury avoiding line at Fairwood Junction with the 09.45 Churston to Paddington on 2 July 1955. R.E.Toop.

With a slight hint of smoke from the chimney and a feather of steam from the safety valves after tackling the ascent from Fairwood Junction, 5053 EARL CAIRNS approaches Clink Road Junction near Frome with the 10.40 from Paddington to Falmouth, on Sunday 22 July 1956. The train is using the stock of the 09.30 weekday down service to Falmouth. R.C.Riley, transporttreasury.co.uk

4009 SHOOTING STAR in perfect condition runs through Frome with the down Torquay Pullman Ltd on 7 June 1930. This short lived service began on 8 July 1929 departing from Paddington at 11.00 on Mondays and Fridays only with intermediate stops at Newton Abbot and Torquay before terminating at Paignton. The corresponding up service departed from Paignton at 16.30 with a booked arrival in Paddington at 20.30. However due to low patronage the train was reduced from eight cars to five in 1930 and the service did not reappear after the end of the 1930 summer timetable. The GWR terminated its contract with the Pullman Car Company in the autumn of the same year. Kidderminster Railway Museum.

Milk trains were once a common sight on the railway system; the Express Dairy Creamery sidings at Frome occupied a cramped location accessed from the up bay platform line used by the Radstock trains.

Frome station with its superb wooden overall roof designed by J.B.Hannaford, one of Brunel's assistants, opened on 7 October 1850. The first train to depart on the opening day was an excursion to Oxford at a cost of 3s 6d. A hundred passengers took advantage and travelled on this train with no less a figure than Daniel Gooch on hand to pilot trains. 41245 has plenty of steam to spare before setting off with a service to Yatton via Witham and Wells on 20 October 1962. Pannier 9612 with loco number chalked on the smokebox door stands on the head shunt to the left. R.C.Riley, transporttreasury.co.uk

The single-road timber engine shed at Frome in July 1956 with 57XX 0-6-0PT 3735 in front, in company with a 2-6-2T. This sub shed of Westbury closed in September 1963. www.railphotoprints.co.uk

7924 THORNYCROFT HALL arrives at Frome with an express service for Weymouth on 30 May 1959. The contraption next to the station sign on the opposite platform is a carriage watering hand pump. Passenger services on the Radstock branch ceased on 31 December 1959. P.J.Garland, Kidderminster Railway Museum.

Top. Witham was the junction for services on the East Somerset line to Shepton Mallet and Wells. 7921 EDSTONE HALL approaches with the 14.15 Weymouth Town-Westbury parcel train on 27 October 1962. C.L.Caddy.

Middle. On a very wet 24 August 1958 5546 stands in the branch bay at Witham after arriving with a train from Wells. The curious timber overall roof for branch line passengers only, which had existed since 1870, was removed in the 1960s. A.E.Bennett, transporttreasury.co.uk

Bottom. 5512 in unlined GWR livery stands in the branch bay at Witham before departing for Wells with a passenger train – the leading coach is an LMS vehicle. Driver, fireman and station staff including the stationmaster pose for the camera in May 1948. 5512 was built in November 1927 and withdrawn in February 1957. J. Moss.

switched out we would continue assisting as far as Witham and return light engine to Castle Cary from there.

Strap Lane Halt with two timber built platforms, just west of Brewham signal box, was served mainly by auto-fitted trains on the Westbury to Taunton local services until closed on 5 June 1950. For all westbound trains the line from Brewham descends for five miles at 1 in 98, a boon for a hard pressed fireman if he had a locomotive that wasn't steaming well, as the long run down the bank would give a chance for the locomotive to rally around. Bruton station generated considerable passenger traffic from the three schools in the town, Kings, Sexeys and Sunny Hill. The small 25 lever Bruton signal box was off the Castle Cary end of the down platform. The goods shed

Top. An all stations stopping train for Weymouth hauled by 4370 has arrived at Witham on 7 May 1932. 5549 has her safety valves lifting in preparation for the journey along the East Somerset branch line to Wells. K.R.M. Kidderminster Railway Museum.

Middle. On a beautiful summers day 6012 KING EDWARD VI runs past the signal box at Brewham on 9 July 1956 with the 15.30 Paddington to Penzance. The train has slipped its Weymouth coaches at Heywood Road Junction, which will be attached to the 16.25 Bristol to Weymouth service at Westbury. R.C.Riley, transporttreasury.co.uk

Bottom. 7017 G.J.CHURCHWARD at Brewham with the second part of the Channel Islands Boat Express at 11.04 on 2 July 1955; the first part, hauled by 6923 CROXTETH HALL had passed the same spot at 10.51. R.C.Riley, transporttreasury.co.uk

Having tackled the steep five-mile long ascent from Castle Cary 6999 CAPEL DEWI HALL runs past the signal box at Brewham with the 09.05 Minehead-Paddington 2 July 1955. When I was a fireman at Yeovil Town one of our duties – see text – involved working a banking engine at night from Castle Cary assisting heavy freight trains to the summit. R.C.Riley, transporttreasury.co.uk

The 08.05 Paddington-Paignton with 5006 TREGENNA CASTLE at Brewham on 2 July 1955. This location was a favourite haunt for photographers in steam days especially on busy summer Saturdays. R.C.Riley, transporttreasury.co.uk

6009 KING CHARLES II with a fair amount of steam leaking from the front end breasts the summit at Brewham on 2 July 1957 with the 08.30 Plymouth-Paddington, which conveyed a slip coach for Reading. R.C.Riley, transporttreasury.co.uk

Left. 5919 WORSLEY HALL in immaculate condition approaches Bruton at speed with an express train for Weymouth on 22 July 1956. This is a good five mile downhill stretch from the summit at Brewham all the way down to Castle Cary. It came in handy if a locomotive was losing steam pressure, affording a chance to rally the steam gauge around. R.C.Riley, transporttreasury.co.uk

Bottom. At Cole the Somerset & Dorset line crossed over the Western Region West of England main line. 3215 proceeds towards Evercreech Junction with a passenger train on 9 June 1962. C.L.Caddy.

on the up side was connected to the up main line by a trailing point at the Castle Cary end of the up platform and to the down main line by a trailing slip connection. There was also a down refuge siding north of the down platform and sidings were provided west of the signal box alongside the down main line.

One mile west of the station, at Cole, the line was crossed by the Bath-Bournemouth section of the Somerset & Dorset Joint Railway; occasionally trains on the Western Region main line running underneath the bridge would coincide with one of the services on the S&D it happened to me one evening when I was firing the Hendford to Westbury goods.

Castle Cary, lying at the foot of the Brewham bank, is the junction for the Weymouth and West of England main lines; trains for the former diverge left after the station taking the original

W.S.&W route at a maximum speed of 30 mph across the junction of the lines, whereas the maximum speed limit for down West of England trains heading for Taunton was 60 mph. Timings for down services through Castle Cary on summer Saturdays in 1957 between 10.03 and 12.17:

09.27	Westbury-Weymouth booked to arrive 10.03 depart at 10.05
07.27	Ealing Broadway-Penzance to pass at 10.11
09.10	Bristol-Weymouth to pass at 10.27
08.10	Paddington-Paignton to pass at 10.34
08.20	Paddington-Weymouth Quay to pass at 10.44
08.25	Paddington-Penzance to pass 10.51
08.30	Paddington-Weymouth Quay to pass at 11.01
08.50	Paddington-Paignton to pass at 11.08
08.30	Weston-super-Mare-Weymouth arr 11.19 dep 11.21
07.50	Birmingham Snow Hill-Weymouth Town to pass 11.27
09.30	Paddington-Newquay to pass 11.33
08.00	Birmingham Snow Hill-Weymouth Town and Quay to pass 11.41
09.40	Paddington-Paignton to pass 11.51
09.35	Paddington-Minehead to pass 12.01
09.34	Reading-Weymouth arr 12.15 dep 12.17.

70017 ARROW runs through Castle Cary with the 09.20 St Ives-Paddington on Saturday 2 July 1955. When summer Saturday traffic was at its peak no less than ten West of England to Paddington express trains were booked to pass through Castle Cary between 13.18 and 15.10 as well as the Weymouth line services. R.C.Riley, transporttreasury.co.uk

Top opposite page. 7018 DRYSLLWYN CASTLE has just passed underneath the Somerset & Dorset line at Cole with the 10.10 Paddington-Penzance pre-summer relief on 9 June 1962. It was a favourite location for photographers and a small group can be seen in the background. C.L.Caddy.

Middle opposite page. Hauling the 11.50 Weymouth-Westbury empty stock on 2 July 1955, 6949 HABERFIELD HALL gets to grip with the ascent to Brewham. This is where the fireman has to get it right. I have fired locomotives on this incline and there is no second chance; apart from a very brief respite in levels at Bruton from then onwards it is a hard slog to the summit. R.C.Riley, transporttreasury.co.uk

Top. A view taken from Castle Cary signal box as 4978 WESTWOOD HALL runs through the station with a down express. It was the scene of a devastating air raid on 3 September 1942, which left three people dead including an engine driver and the signalman, with ten people injured. Adrian Vaughan collection.

Middle. 4917 CROSSWOOD HALL in immaculate condition and without a sign of steam from the front end, arrives at Castle Cary with the 11.12 Weymouth-Paddington on 2 July 1955. The three signals on the gantry read from left to right: down refuge, down Weymouth, down main; the ringed signal in the background controls the exit from the down goods loop. R.C.Riley, transporttreasury.co.uk

Below. 4918 DARTINGTON HALL diverges from the West of England main line and takes the Weymouth route at Castle Cary with a down express on 22 July 1956. The signal box in the background replaced the previous box destroyed by enemy bombing in 1942. R.C.Riley, transporttreasury.co.uk

This is but a small part of the westbound Saturday services through the station and delays however small would cause a ripple effect through the system. For example, trains delayed by adverse signals at Taunton would not have the speed to pick up water at Creech water troughs and therefore would stop at Castle Cary for water. Ahead of them was the ascent to Brewham now from a dead stand; likewise down trains having a similar problem at Fairwood Junction and booked to run via the Frome avoiding line would take the chance to fill up with water at Castle Cary.

A fairly level run followed, through the stations at Sparkford and Marston Magna before the approach to Yeovil Pen Mill, a station protected by distant signals permanently fixed at caution and speed restrictions through both platform

Top. BR Standard 5MT 4-6-0 73029 takes to the Weymouth line at Castle Cary with a lengthy freight train on 7 July 1959. R.C.Riley, transporttreasury.co.uk

Middle. 1012 COUNTY OF DENBIGH runs through Sparkford with the up Channel Islands Boat train on 31 August 1959. H.B.Priestley.

Below. 6960 RAVENINGHAM HALL arrives at Yeovil Pen Mill with an express for Weymouth on 23 August 1958. When working an ex-GWR locomotive down from Westbury the station at Yeovil was the only place where the platform was on the driver's side of the locomotive. A.E.Bennett, transporttreasury.co.uk

lines. This, combined with the adverse gradient west of the station to Evershot, soon developed a bottleneck if services were running late. Most if not all Weymouth services stopped at Yeovil, although there were exceptions. The maximum speed limit for down through trains was 30 mph, and down services booked to run through non-stop included the 08.20, 08.30 and 21.30 ex-Paddington. The 08.20 and 08.30 were timed through at 11.00 and 11.16 respectively and the sixteen minute gap between the two trains was generous provided the 08.20 was running on time and had a good journey up the Evershot bank, for which assistance would be

Top. Steam issues from the cylinders and safety valves of 5996 MYTTON HALL hauling a Paddington to Weymouth express at Yeovil Pen Mill on 10 July 1956. R.C.Riley, transporttreasury.co.uk

Middle. 6945 GLASFRYN HALL has plenty of steam to spare at Yeovil Pen Mill with a Swindon Works-Weymouth holiday special on 10 July 1956. Known to legions of workers as 'The Trip' this annual event occurred in July of each year when the locomotive works at Swindon closed for two weeks. A masterpiece of organisation, when every worker had their accommodation and train booked for themselves and their families. R.C.Riley, transporttreasury.co.uk

Bottom. 3737 stands in the down yard at Yeovil Pen Mill, this was a busy freight yard handling large amounts of goods traffic to the main shunting yard at Hendford on the western side of Yeovil and transfer freights to Yeovil Junction which were tripped via Yeovil Town station. James Harrold, transporttreasury.co.uk

YEOVIL
OS Map 1928 Crown Copyright Reserved

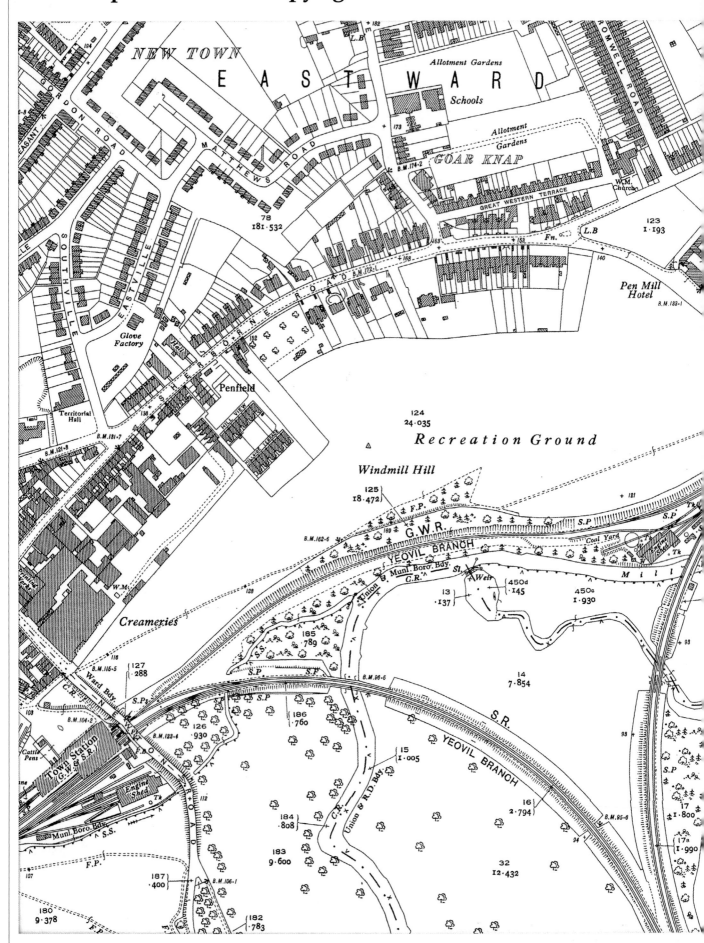

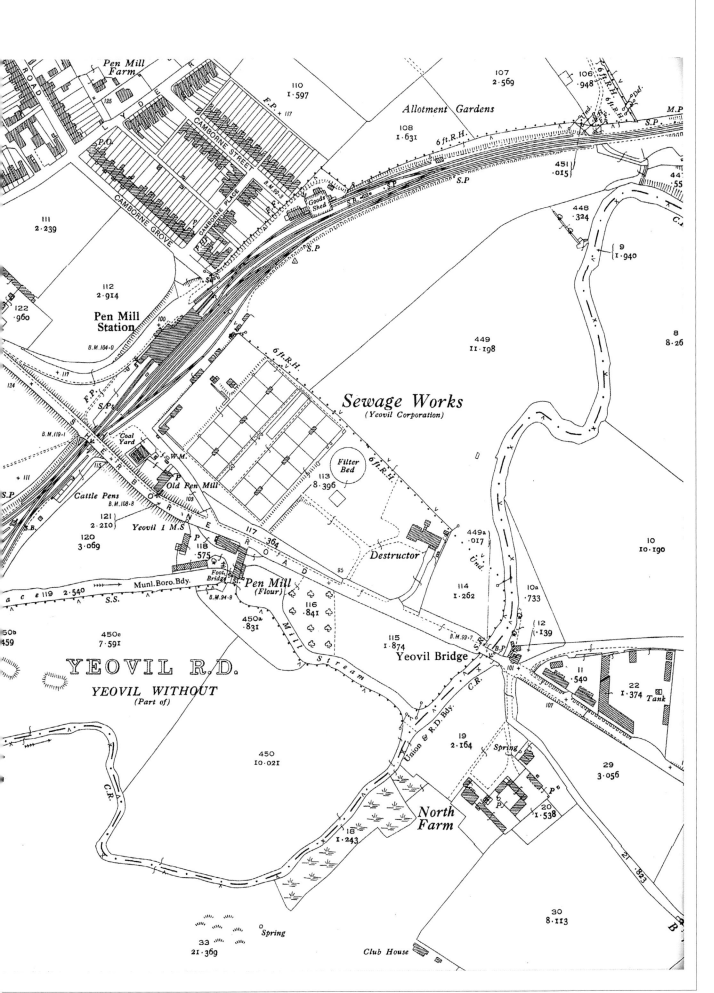

3816 with a freight train for Weymouth at Yeovil Pen Mill. All down freights stopped here to replenish the tender, drop off and pick up wagons and attach an assisting engine (instead of Yetminster) for the ascent to Evershot. www.railphotoprints.

6945 GLASFRYN HALL slows for the speed restriction through the up platform at Pen Mill with a Weymouth to Westbury service in 1957. C.L.Caddy.

provided from Yetminster. The speed restriction for up trains from Weymouth was more severe at 10 mph, due to the dog-leg curve at the Weymouth end of the up platform. Trains arriving from Weymouth and booked to run through included the 09.25 Wolverhampton, 10.00 Birmingham Moor Street, 11.05 ECS to Westbury, 13.35 Cardiff and 15.45 Paddington.

Yeovil Pen Mill station was also the starting and termination point for trains to Taunton via Yeovil Town and the branch line to Langport West, with a service of approximately eight trains each way. Unusually, compared with other stations on the route from Paddington, there was no separate bay platform for the branch trains; all arrived at the up platform which was bi-directionally signalled, enabling a branch loco to run round and depart from the same platform (to Taunton) after arrival from Yeovil Town station. At times the branch trains were started from the down platform, if conflicting movements occurred, but in any case the congested nature of the layout meant that slick moves were sometimes required. For example, the 17.50 from Taunton would arrive via Yeovil Town at 19.05 occupying the up platform; meanwhile the 18.10 Weymouth-Westbury would be approaching with a booked arrival of 19.15 The ex-Taunton service would be quickly emptied of passengers and shunted into the down yard clear of the 17.02 Bristol-Weymouth due in at 19.10 which was also booked to take water at

the down platform, and when the 17.02 had departed, the branch train would return to the down platform to form the 19.50 to Taunton.

A total of seventeen down Weymouth and twelve up trains, plus local railmotors, were booked to stop at the station on a summer Saturday. Delays would always occur with late running services and locomotive failures were rare. They were alas not unknown of course and if they did happen would put a spanner well and truly in the works, for example when 5082 SWORDFISH was in trouble on the down Channel Islands Boat Express. The errant Castle was replaced at Yeovil by U Class 2-6-0 31802 from the Southern's Yeovil Town shed and was hauled there to have the fire dropped, to be dragged back to the Western Region by a locomotive sent especially down from Westbury a few days later.

The former GWR Yeovil Pen Mill engine shed occupied the vee of land created by the Weymouth main line on one side and the single-track branch to Yeovil Town on the other. It was a simple three-road timber building with a brick office, plus a coaling platform and small turntable at the rear alongside the branch to Yeovil Town. The allocation was made up in the main of ten or so tank locomotives used on double or treble shifts for banking duties at Evershot and Castle Cary, passenger and freight trains on the Taunton branch, shunting at Pen Mill and Hendford Goods Yards, plus various trip workings along the

Westbury-Weymouth line and at one time a passenger working to Bristol. The final allocation upon closure in January 1959 when the locos and crews were transferred to the Southern Region shed at Yeovil Town comprised two 45XX 'small prairies' and half a dozen 57XX panniers.

The layout west of Yeovil Pen Mill station, from the A30 road bridge on 10 July 1956; 2-6-2T 5542 stands on the down Weymouth main line. The route to Yeovil Town curves away to the right becoming single track around the corner. The engine shed complete with turntable had an allocation of ten tank locomotives in 1950. R.C.Riley, transporttreasury.co.uk

Above. Pannier tank 1881 standing outside Pen Mill shed on 13 July 1936 ; it was built as a saddle tank at Swindon Works in December 1890 and altered in November 1918. F.K.Davies, Kidderminster Railway Museum.

Top right. 5548 in the yard at Pen Mill shed; note the short-lived right facing lion of the later BR crest (only a left facing lion was authorised, by the College of Heralds, for both sides). This locomotive was allocated to Yeovil Town shed upon the closure of Pen Mill in 1959. I have worked on the footplate of 5548 more than once, either working trains on the branch to Taunton, or on banking duties at Evershot and Castle Cary. Kidderminster Railway Museum.

Right. South of Yeovil Pen Mill the Weymouth main line ran alongside the Southern Region Yeovil Town branch for a short distance at Yeovil South Junction. Drummond M7 0-4-4T 30129 propels 'Ironclad' push & pull set No.383 forming the 12.36 Yeovil Town-Yeovil Junction on 3 January 1959. The through Waterloo coach at the rear will be attached to a Salisbury-bound train at Yeovil Junction and upon arrival at Salisbury will be attached to the up Atlantic Coast Express. The ex-GWR Weymouth tracks are on the far right. J.J.Smith Collection, Bluebell Railway Museum.

82E Yeovil Pen Mill
Bristol Division
Shed Code 82E (1949-1958) 71H (1958-1959)
Locomotive Allocations 1950
Total locomotives – 10

Class 57XX 0-6-0PT
3671, 3733, 4689, 5767, 8745, 9601, 9732/71

Class 45XX 2-6-2T
5529/65

7908 HENSHALL HALL runs past Thornford Bridge Halt with the 08.00 Birmingham-Weymouth Quay boat train on 7 July 1962. The maximum loading for this class of locomotive working trains unassisted to Evershot was 288 tons. C.L.Caddy.

5563 complete with a patched side tank stands in readiness for banking duties at Yetminster on 7 July 1962. Note the BR emblem is in its proper form when compared with an earlier photograph of 5548 at Yeovil Pen Mill shed. C.L.Caddy.

Chapter 4
Yeovil to Weymouth

Trains bound for Weymouth would now be heading towards the worst part of their journey, for the crews at least. This was the ascent to Evershot. First came the run alongside the Yeovil Town-Yeovil Junction branch from Yeovil South Junction (where a connection between the GWR and the Southern complete with a signal box opened during the Second World War) south to run under the Southern West of England main line. After passing Thornford Bridge Halt all down trains requiring assistance would stop at Yetminster. The station lies at the foot of the climb at 1 in 51 for 5½ miles to the summit at Evershot. The banking engines would be waiting in the down refuge siding near the signal box and would be released on to the rear of the waiting train when it had arrived. We wouldn't couple up, but instead just pushed up to the rear of the train with buffers compressed, ready to go, and awaiting the loco at the front of the train to whistle up. This would be a 'cock a doodle' type of call, the response on our whistle would be exactly the same, and at that moment both locomotives would move, with both on full regulator to have a good crack at the bank.

Chetnole Halt, two miles south-west of Yetminster had staggered timber platforms, either side of an adjacent road bridge. Holywell Tunnel 308 yards long is at the summit of the 1 in 51 ascent from Yetminster and many footplate crews in the steam era including myself, were pleased to see the tunnel mouth come into view especially if they had been having a rough trip up the bank. Upon arrival at the summit at Evershot the banking locomotives would be switched

Left. **4918 DARTINGTON HALL** in immaculate condition and with electrification warning signs on the boiler cladding and firebox (it must have been in danger recently of venturing on to the electrified LMR) nears Holywell Tunnel at the summit of the 5½ mile long Evershot bank with the 10.00 Swindon-Weymouth excursion on 14 August 1960. The locomotive is just passing over the catch point, which is intended to derail any wagons that may have broken away from a train. S.C.Nash, Courtesy of The Stephenson Locomotive Society.

Below. **1009 COUNTY OF CARMARTHEN** ascends the Evershot bank near Chetnole on 14 August 1960 with the 09.38 Bristol Parson Street-Weymouth. S.C.Nash, Courtesy Stephenson Locomotive Society.

across to the up main by the signalman and, after refilling with water from the column at the end of the up platform, would return to Yetminster. Evershot station was 500ft above sea level and unusual in that the buildings were in timber. In its early years the Lord and Lady Ilchester had the right to have a passenger train stopped at their convenience.

The hardest part of the journey for steam locomotive crews was now over, and with the descent to Maiden Newton they could take things easier. Cattistock Halt, four miles beyond Evershot, was a two-platform timber built affair, served mainly by auto trains on the Yeovil-

Top. The fireman of 73017 waves on the approach to Evershot station with a Weymouth-Westbury train of perishables from the Channel Islands on 28 May 1960. John Day.

Middle. After arriving at Evershot with a Yeovil to Weymouth Auto train in September 1929 the fireman of 517 class 0-4-2T 542 stands on the boiler to get the water 'bag' in place. This locomotive was built at Wolverhampton Works in 1869 as a saddle tank and converted to side tanks in 1880. Auto apparatus was fitted in October 1923 and the locomotive was withdrawn from service in April 1934. Dr. Ian C.Allen, transporttreasury.co.uk

Bottom. Named after a GWR Director and son of one of the two founders of the Cunard Line, Bulldog class 4-4-0 3369 DAVID MAC IVER stands in the up goods yard at Evershot in September 1929 whilst working a Weymouth-Westbury freight. The bulk of the train has been left on the main line and the locomotive has entered the yard to pick up or drop off wagons. Dr Ian C.Allen, transporttreasury.co.uk

Weymouth services. A little further on came the prettily-named Maiden Newton, junction for the 9¼ mile line to Bridport. Trains on the branch services used a bay alongside the up platform, provided with a timber overall roof after the fashion of the one at Witham. There were no conventional run round arrangements; instead, the locomotive, a pannier or 'small prairie' made use of a gravity shunt siding. The loco pushed the stock into this siding and while it took water the guard, on the coach handbrake, allowed the branch train to trundle into place for the return to Bridport.

Top. 3815 COUNTY OF HANTS with a Birmingham to Weymouth express at Evershot in September 1929. Following on from the previous photograph of DAVID MAC IVER note the ground disc signal is 'off' and the shunter is walking away from the camera towards the wagons being pulled out of the siding and on to the main line, whereupon the wagons will be coupled to the rest of the train for the journey to Yeovil. Dr Ian C.Allen, transporttreasury.co.uk

Middle. 7917 NORTH ASTON HALL pulls away from Maiden Newton towards Evershot with the 14.15 Weymouth to Swindon parcels train on 24 July 1958. The ascent to Evershot from here although severe, is never as demanding on a crew and locomotive as the climb from Yetminster. R.C.Riley, transporttreasury.co.uk

Bottom. Reflecting the days when the Weymouth route was a main line in its own right. 5034 CORFE CASTLE runs through Maiden Newton with a down Channel Islands boat express on 4 September 1959. H.B.Priestley.

The line is now running south-east, to Frampton Tunnel (660yds long) and then Grimstone & Frampton station, two platforms joined by a footbridge. There was a 20 lever signal box off the Dorchester end of the up platform. Bradford Peverell & Stratton Halt was next, with its 150ft staggered timber platforms serving the two villages in its title, each about half a mile away.

Top. There were no run around facilities at Maiden Newton for trains arriving from Bridport and once the handful of passengers had decamped the locomotive, like 'small prairie' 4507 here, would reverse its coaches up a small gravity siding, uncouple, run forward and then reverse along the line to the right to refill with water from the adjacent column. Meanwhile the guard would release the hand brake and the stock would roll into the bay platform under gravity. James Harrold, transporttreasury.co.uk

Middle. The Bridport branch bay at Maiden Newton (as at Witham for the East Somerset trains) had an attractive timber built train shed in the Brunelian style. 14XX 0-4-2T 1474 is ready to leave for the next trip to Bridport. Although this engine is auto-fitted I cannot recollect seeing auto-trains working along the branch. James Harrold, transporttreasury.co.uk

Bottom. Mogul 5384 pulls away from Dorchester West with a Weymouth-Westbury freight; the line was well served by freight trains with seven scheduled weekday services running between Paddington, Bristol, Westbury, Yeovil, Swindon and Reading. 5384, built at Swindon in July 1920, was withdrawn from service in October 1960. James Harrold, transporttreasury.co.uk

After Poundbury Tunnel came Dorchester West and its 29 lever signal box and, beyond, Dorchester Junction where the ex-LSWR, Southern Region lines from Dorchester South and Waterloo come in from the east. There was a 40 mph speed restriction in place in BR days for trains to and from the Westbury route across the junction, controlled by the 36 lever Dorchester Junction signal box in the fork of the two lines.

Monkton & Came Halt with its two timber platforms served the inhabitants of the nearby village of Winterborne Monkton; after that came Bincombe Tunnel signal box, alongside the up main line complete with an engine siding for banking locomotives awaiting the road back to Weymouth.

Top. The fireman of 5924 DINTON HALL gazes at the photographer whilst working the 17.20 Weymouth-Bristol passenger train at Dorchester West on 1 August 1963. As a fireman I always disliked having my photograph taken while working on the footplate, and would always move out of shot if I happened to notice a photographer approaching our locomotive. Dorchester West signal box in the background. Ron F. Smith, transporttreasury.co.uk

Middle. 5997 SPARKFORD HALL arrives at Dorchester West with the 09.00 (SO) Weymouth-Paddington in April 1956. Trains were well loaded during this era, especially at weekends when there were great numbers of HM forces personnel on leave or returning to the various military bases in the area including the large Royal Navy establishment at Portland. C.L.Caddy.

Bottom. The 09.15 Swindon-Weymouth parcels with 4918 DARTINGTON HALL in ex-works condition, standing alongside the down platform at Dorchester West on 16 August 1960. H.B.Priestley.

The line now runs downhill at a gradient of 1 in 52 for four miles, through the 814 yard long Bincombe Tunnel, through the short tunnel under the main Dorchester-Weymouth road and then past Upwey Wishing Well Halt; another pretty name on a line replete with pretty names. Upwey & Broadwey, formerly known as Upwey Junction, was junction for the 8¼ mile long branch to Abbotsbury which had closed to passengers on 1 December 1952, though a short section remained open for freight until 1962. Radipole Halt on the outskirts of Weymouth was one of 51 Halts opened by the GWR in 1905.

Weymouth engine shed was laid out north of the station alongside the down

Top. An unidentified Modified Hall is signalled for the Yeovil line at Dorchester Junction with an up boat train from Weymouth in August 1949. There was a speed limit of 40 mph here for trains using the ex-GWR route through Dorchester West. S.V.Blencowe.

Middle. 6985 PARWICK HALL near Dorchester just south of the site of the closed Monkton & Came Halt, hauling a troop train formed of Southern Region stock on 11 August 1963. C.L.Caddy.

Bottom. 5978 BODINNICK HALL blasts out of the short 56 yard long South tunnel at Bincombe with the 14.30 Weymouth-Westbury stopping train on 31 May 1950. The longer North tunnel is behind the photographer. J.C.Flemons, transporttreasury.co.uk

main; it dated from June 1885 and had replaced an earlier cramped two-road shed from the 1850s, near to the station. The new shed was built to the Dean pattern, the generation before Churchward and with four roads was constructed in brick with a northlight pattern roof. A new 65ft turntable replacing the old 50ft one appeared in 1925 and a new coal stage in 1930. The shed had an allocation of about thirty ex-GWR locomotives in 1950 including 2912

Top. Lord Nelson 4-6-0 30864 SIR MARTIN FROBISHER runs downhill from Bincombe North tunnel with a Bournemouth to Weymouth service on 31 May 1950. Underneath the grime the locomotive is in 1948 experimental Apple Green livery. The wooden arm lower quadrant signal on the left with a distinctive lean is the Bincombe Tunnel signal box up distant. J.C.Flemons, transporttreasury.co.uk

Middle. 73065 heading the 15.50 Weymouth-Waterloo on 27 March 1967, near the entrance to the 814 yard long North tunnel at Bincombe. This was a ghastly place always full of noxious gases, steam and smoke, and the only way to gauge if we were moving forward, slipping or standing still, was to reach out from the footplate and touch the tunnel wall with the firing shovel. Note the 'wonky' ex-GWR distant signal in the previous picture has been replaced by a Southern Region upper quadrant signal arm and post. John Bird, SOUTHERN-IMAGES

Bottom. The Channel Islands Boat train services to Weymouth were transferred in 1959 to the Southern Region route from Waterloo. 73110 (with nameplates removed) coasts downhill out of Bincombe North tunnel with the boat train from Waterloo on 5 May 1965. C.L.Caddy

Clear signals ahead for 6945 GLASFRYN HALL with the 16.10 Weymouth-Paddington at Upwey Junction on 31 May 1950. The train was booked to stop at Frome to drop off mail and intending passengers for Bristol from Weymouth and the Channel Islands whereupon they would travel via Radstock and the North Somerset line. The oncoming train is the 14.57 Bournemouth Central-Weymouth hauled by 30859 LORD HOOD. J.C.Flemons, transporttreasury.co.uk

A 14XX 0-4-2T after arrival at Upwey Junction from the Abbotsbury branch line (diverging to the far left) propels its auto-trailer onto the down main line heading for Weymouth on 31 May 1950. The two signal arms on the GWR bracket signal control access to the branch (left arm) with the taller signal the up main inner home. J.C.Flemons, transporttreasury.co.uk

Top. 73018 working a Weymouth-Eastleigh freight train approaches Upwey & Broadwey on 11 August 1963. The old Abbotsbury branch (in the foreground) by now is now a truncated stub leading to Upwey Goods. C.L.Caddy.

Middle. Upwey & Broadwey station and its attractive footbridge linking the platforms, looking north on 30 March 1961. The main station building, in timber, is on the left, complete with a corrugated iron lamp room. The former Abbotsbury branch trains used the platform behind. Thomas Hardy wrote a poem here, *At the Railway Station Upway* whilst waiting for a train. It was renamed Upwey in 1980 and is served today by First Great Western between Bristol Temple Meads and Weymouth and South West Trains on the Waterloo/Bournemouth/Weymouth route. John Eyers, South Western Circle.

Bottom. One of Eastleigh's Class 4 2-6-0s, 76025 at Upwey & Broadwey with the 12.10 Weymouth-Bournemouth Central on 30 March 1961. The station had opened as Upwey Junction on 19 April 1886. The six mile branch to Abbotsbury opened on 9 November 1885 and as the new station (Upwey Junction) was not ready, all trains from Abbotsbury had to proceed to Weymouth. Upwey Junction had been renamed Upwey & Broadwey from 29 November 1952, the Abbotsbury branch closed to passenger traffic on 1 December 1952 with most of the track lifted by 1955 except for the section between the junction and the former Upwey station (renamed Upwey Goods) on the branch line which was reduced to a siding for freight only. John Eyers, South Western Circle.

Top. Upwey and Broadway station from the down platform on 30 March 1961, looking towards Weymouth with the junction for the former Abbotsbury branch line (by now a siding for Upwey Goods) can be seen at the far right in the distance. Freight traffic mainly for the local coal merchant at Upwey Goods lingered on until 1 January 1962, the branch stub and connections to the main line were taken out of use on 7 July 1963. Upwey and Broadway became unstaffed from 1 March 1965. John Eyers, South Western Circle.

Middle. Upwey and Broadway station as viewed from the footbridge, looking towards Weymouth on 30 March 1961. The 22 lever signal box at the end of the down platform opened as 'Upwey Junction' on 9 November 1885 and was renamed along with the station to 'Upwey and Broadway' from 29 November 1952. The box was taken out of use on 1 March 1970. The original GWR station buildings were demolished and replaced by bus stop type shelters although the footbridge remains. John Eyers, South Western Circle.

Bottom. Casting a pall with the fireman getting his fire right for the 1 in 51 climb to Bincombe and the safety valves lifting indicating plenty of steam 6838, devoid of nameplate, heads the 09.25 (SO) Weymouth-Wolverhampton through the former Upwey Junction (renamed Upwey & Broadway in November 1952). Another locomotive is giving assistance at the rear of the train. C.L.Caddy.

Driver and fireman of GWR 517 class 0-4-2T 202 pose for the camera near Radipole with an Abbotsbury-Weymouth goods, consisting of an empty open wagon and brake van, on 7 August 1901. C.H.Eden, Kidderminster Railway Museum.

3386 PADDINGTON departs from Weymouth *circa* 1921 at the head of an express passenger train of Dean clerestory roofed stock. The Bulldog class appeared on the route in the early years of the twentieth century monopolising the faster Weymouth services by replacing the 4-4-0 Duke class designed by William Dean. The best GWR train from Weymouth to Paddington by 1924 took three hours forty minutes, which was 15 minutes longer than the rival Southern Railway service to Waterloo. R.Brookman, Kidderminster Railway Museum.

WEYMOUTH
OS Map 1959 Crown Copyright reserved

SAINT AMBROSE, 4080 POWDERHAM CASTLE and nine Halls. All this was vastly different in 1965 when the allocation consisted of twelve rebuilt Merchant Navy Pacifics, six Class 5MT 4-6-0s and five Class 2MT 2-6-2Ts.

What had happened to bring this about was a number of boundary alterations between the SR and WR

enacted in 1957, to 'restore conformity between Regions and Operating Areas in the South West.' The WR got the Somerset and Dorset for instance, but the Southern Region took over Yeovil Pen Mill, Bridport and Weymouth sheds, along with the line from Dorchester to Weymouth of course. The Weymouth shed code changed from 82F to 71G and all its 25 locos – the 'dockie'

1366 panniers, some moguls, 'big' and 'small' prairies, panniers, four 0-4-2Ts and five Halls, were transferred to the SR. Little changed for a few years but as the 1960s drew on the former GW locos disappeared.

Weymouth Junction, just north of Weymouth station, was the diverging point for trains using the Portland and Weymouth Quay lines. The Quay line

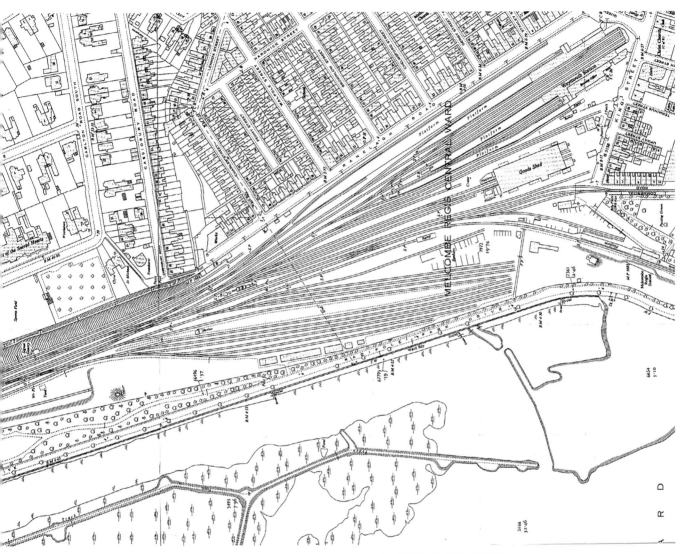

Approaching journeys end, 6319 with a down train displaying class A headlamps at Radipole Halt on 11 May 1963. C.L.Caddy.

itself was a branch off the Portland line until directly connected to the main line in later years. After arrival in Weymouth Yard the engine, restaurant car, leading brake and any coaches for Weymouth Town were detached from boat trains and the rest hauled along the tramway to Weymouth Quay by one of the little 1366 pannier tanks, all of which were equipped with a warning bell, to be operated by the fireman when the train was in motion between Weymouth Yard and the Quay. The procession would also be accompanied by shunters with red flags to control the road traffic. They were required to walk 30-50 yards in front of the train warning road traffic of its approach; a unique sight to see scheduled main line passenger trains trundling through streets past parked cars at four miles per hour.

Top. 30785 SIR MADOR DE LA PORTE in Malachite Green livery arrives at Weymouth with a passenger service from Bournemouth Central on 31 May 1950. This locomotive was one of a batch of thirty of the class built by the North British Locomotive Company, hence the nickname 'Scotch Arthurs'. J.C.Flemons, transporttreasury.co.uk

Middle. 5091 CLEEVE ABBEY arrives at Weymouth with a boat train from Birmingham on 25 July 1964. The tracks in the foreground mark the entry/exit to the engine shed; a locomotive fresh off shed and awaiting permission to run tender first into the station can be seen to the right just past the signal gantry. C.L.Caddy.

Bottom. 7782 has arrived from Portland on 4 July 1963 with a freight service and the train will now be split and remarshalled for destinations far and wide. C.L.Caddy.

82F Weymouth

Bristol Division
Shed Code 82F (1949-1958) 71G
(1958-1963) 70G (1963-1967)
Locomotive Allocations 1950
Total locomotives – 31

Class 1366 0-6-0PT
1367, 1368,1370

Class 14XX 0-4-2T
1453,1453,1454,1467

Class 1501 0-6-0PT
1789

Saint 4-6-0
2912

Castle 4-6-0
4080

Class 45XX 2-6-2T
4507, 4520, 4527, 4562

Hall 4-6-0
4930, 4988, 5968, 5978, 6902, 6912,
6945, 6988, 6993

Class 43XX 2-6-0
5305, 5314, 5328, 3738, 3759, 3784

Class 74XX 0-6-0PT
7408

Class 57XX 0-6-0PT
9642

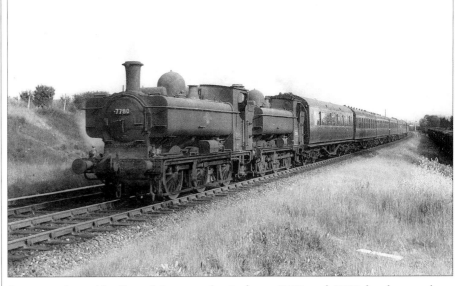

An unusual combination of two pannier tanks as 7780 and 7782 head away from Weymouth with a return excursion to Yeovil on 11 June 1962. Both locomotives were allocated to Weymouth shed and the pairing may be the result of the failure of the booked locomotive; generally, the excursion trains between Yeovil and Weymouth were worked by Yeovil crews and locomotives. C.L.Caddy.

Weymouth shed on 1 August 1963 with the Jersey sidings in the foreground and the main lines in the middle of the picture. Two BR 5MT 4-6-0s stand at the entrance of the shed, by a lone Hymek diesel. These first appeared on regular services on 16 September 1961, hauling the 10.10 (SO) Bristol-Weymouth and returning with the 15.25 to Bristol. Photograph H.F.Wheeler.

The tramway was worked without signals or block telegraph, under a time interval system, supervised by an inspector assisted by a shunter in charge and a shunter. Passenger trains were restricted to twelve coaches and 70ft coaches were banned. Vast amounts of market garden produce shipped in from France and the Channel Islands were transported by rail, the main traffic being flowers, tomatoes and potatoes from the Channel Islands and broccoli from France. An unexpected boost to passenger and freight traffic came in 1960 when the Southern Region withdrew shipping facilities between Southampton and the

Top. With the engine shed in the background, 76011 arrives at Weymouth with the 12.53 from Bournemouth Central on 30 March 1961. The BR 4MT 2-6-0s comprised a total of 115 locomotives built in the BR Works at Horwich (45), Doncaster (25) and Derby (45). John Eyers, South Western Circle.

Right. Weymouth looking towards the station on 30 March 1961 with 4624 standing on the up main line and 1367 in the sidings on the right. 1367 was allocated to Weymouth in April 1935 to work the boat trains between the harbour and Weymouth Junction and by 1947 1368 and 1370 had also arrived. All three were fitted with a warning bell for working along the tramway, plus a footplate step and handrail on the front right-hand side for the shunters. John Eyers, South Western Circle.

Below. 2978 CHARLES J HAMBRO taking water at Weymouth shed in June 1937 after working a train from the Westbury line. The locomotive carried the name KIRKLAND until May 1935. A.P Dowley, Kidderminster Railway Museum.

Top. 4143 from Taunton shed stands on the disposal pit after working a Taunton-Weymouth excursion on 24 June 1962. The train had travelled an interesting route from Taunton, along the West of England main line to Curry Rivel junction then diverging on to the old Bristol & Exeter branch line via Langport West and Martock to Yeovil Pen Mill where the locomotive would have run around its train to complete the journey to Weymouth. Two rebuilt Bulleid Pacifics stand in the background, already turned, with tenders refilled with coal and water for their next trip to Waterloo. C.L.Caddy.

Middle. 6304 reverses on to the Weymouth 65ft turntable on 13 April 1963. When the shed opened in 1885 it was equipped with a 49ft 9in turntable, by 1920 it had been fitted with extension bars in order to turn the larger locomotives then appearing. It was removed and replaced by this 65ft turntable repositioned at the end of the shed yard. C.L.Caddy.

Bottom. 5094 TRETOWER CASTLE has been turned, watered and coaled in readiness for a run back to Paddington on 27 June 1951. Weymouth closed with the end of steam on the Southern on 9 July 1967, though a signing-on point remained in use until October 1970. R.S.Carpenter.

Weymouth in 1949; dating from 20 January 1857 the timber built terminus with its overall roof and glazed end screens was designed by T.H.Bertram, one of Brunel's assistants and constructed at a cost of £10,000. Plans were mooted in 1935 to reconstruct the station, but were halted due to the onset of the Second World War; the glass was removed from the roof in 1939 as an air raid precaution. The roof was removed in 1951, followed by new platforms and a new signal box replacing the former junction and station boxes in 1957. J.Moss.

Weymouth on 30 March 1961; platform 1 on the far right, looking towards the buffer stops. With the opening of the improved platforms and new signal box in 1957, all platforms were available for both arrivals and departures, although it remained the practice to use Nos.1, 2 and 3 for departures, with 3 as the main departure platform and 2 dealing with most of the Southern Region trains. No.1 was devoid of shelter, inconvenient for the ticket collectors and only used about three times per day. On the arrival side, as many trains as possible ran into 4, leaving 5 as the parcels platform and partially occupied for most of the day with bogie vans. This practice ceased around 1961 and thereafter No.6 was used by arriving passenger trains when space was limited due to excursion traffic. When the local services went over to DMU working, the units tended to arrive at 1, 2 or 3 ready to form the return service. John Eyers, South Western Circle.

Above. An early morning at Weymouth in September 1966. John Eyers, courtesy South Western Circle.

Left. 4992 CROSBY HALL, issuing a smoky trail over the station before departure with an up express, was just over one year old when this picture was taken at Weymouth on 31 August 1932. Kidderminster Railway Museum.

Below. The fire of Saint class 4-6-0 2981 IVANHOE is under perfect control without a breath of smoke issuing from the chimney before departure from Weymouth on 13 July 1929 with an express for Paddington. Note the clerestory carriage in the background displaying the GWR coat of arms, and the fine gas lamp near the seat on the platform. Kidderminster Railway Museum.

The fireman of 2902 LADY OF THE LAKE trims and refills the headlamps after arrival at Weymouth on 13 July 1929. He will then leave one lamp on the bracket to act as a tail lamp whilst travelling tender first to the shed. The Southern Railway gas tank No.66S alongside was used for filling the tanks on restaurant cars, for cooking. Kidderminster Railway Museum.

Channel Islands to concentrate the traffic on Weymouth.

Long fully-fitted trains designated 'Per Pots' conveying produce from the Channel Islands laboured over the gradients of the old GWR route to Westbury and beyond with ever increasing frequency. Up to five a day departed from the Quay and additional sidings were provided at Weymouth and on the tramway to deal with the extra traffic. Holiday traffic and market produce increased dramatically during the 1950s with four or sometimes five boat trains arriving on summer Saturdays.

Sailings from Weymouth Quay to the Channel Islands were handled for many years by the *St. Helier* and *St. Julian* supplemented at weekends by the larger and more modern *St. Patrick*. The two smaller ships had a capacity of 950 passengers, whilst the *St. Patrick* could carry 1,300. The 13.00 sailing to the Channel Islands due in Jersey at 19.00 was followed on summer Saturdays by an additional sailing at 13.30 by the *St. Patrick* which returned overnight to Weymouth, arriving at 06.00. The greatest demand was for the 13.00 sailing from Weymouth Quay, as this was the connection out of the London boat trains. Mid-week excursions to Guernsey operated by *St. Patrick* were very popular, departing from the Quay at 09.30 arriving in Guernsey at 13.30; the fare was 25 shillings return.

The last Channel Islands Boat Train from Paddington ran on 26 September 1959 with services transferred to the Waterloo route, although a portion from Weymouth Quay was conveyed on the 16.10 to Paddington on Tuesdays, Thursdays and Saturdays from 29 September to 31 October 1959; the down portion for the Quay arrived attached to the 18.00 from Paddington.

Weymouth Town station during the 1950s on summer Saturdays was a hive of activity with holidaymakers arriving and departing either via the Western route to Paddington, Birmingham, Wolverhampton and Bristol or via the Southern to Waterloo. Excursion traffic was also at its peak in the 1950s with extra trains arriving on summer Sundays from far and wide. The station saw a number of alterations under BR. The original building was designed by T.H. Bertram and constructed in timber with an overall roof across the tracks; in poor condition (the glass had been removed from the roof in 1939 as a precaution against air raids) the roof was demolished in 1951. In 1957 two lengthy excursion platforms, 5 and 6 (both of which are incorporated into the present station) were added. Each one could hold a twelve-coach train and the layout was improved to allow all six platforms to be used by either arrivals or departures. Additional sidings were laid adjacent to Jubilee Gardens and a new 116 lever signal box replaced the two old GWR boxes. With opening of the new signalbox, all six platforms were now available for both arrivals and departures, although

it remained the practice to use Nos.1, 2 and 3 for departures and 4, 5 and 6 for arrivals. No.3 was the main departure platform, with No.2 dealing with most of the Southern Region trains. No.1 was devoid of shelter and only used about three times a day.

On the arrival side as many trains as possible were run into No.4 with No.6 the next choice; No.5 was the parcels platform and partially occupied for much of the day with van traffic. This changed about 1961 and No.6 became the parcels platform and thereafter only used by passenger trains when excursions were pouring in at weekends. When the local services went over to DMUs, the units would tend to arrive at 1, 2, or 3 ready to form the return service.

Postscript

The golden years which had seen traffic levels soar after the end of the Second World War were becoming a memory in the 1960s, to the detriment of the GWR route. The two daily return trains between Paddington and Weymouth were reduced to one each way from 13 June 1960, to a down train only from 12 September of the same year, and withdrawn completely on 11 September 1961. DMUs had appeared on the route from 6 April 1959 working a total of three up and down services a day, interspersed with the steam workings, but steam remained in charge of freight and parcels traffic as well as some of the longer distance trains.

From 16 September 1961 the first regular diesel locomotives appeared with Hymek Type 3 diesels working the 10.10 (SO) Bristol-Weymouth and returning with the 15.25 from Weymouth. More reductions came in 1966 with general freight trains withdrawn between Castle Cary and Weymouth on the introduction of the summer timetable. Although some Channel Island produce trains continued to use the route, many were diverted via Bournemouth, Southampton and Reading. From 3 October 1966 the stations and halts at Witham, Sparkford, Marston Magna, Evershot, Cattistock, Grimstone & Frampton and Bradford & Peverell were closed; more retraction came in 1968 when the line between Castle Cary and Dorchester West was singled with passing loops provided at Yeovil Pen Mill and Maiden Newton.

The cargo service between Weymouth and the Channel Islands was withdrawn in the 1970s making much of the Jubilee and Jersey sidings redundant. Weymouth station was progressively rationalised after the end of steam in 1967, the goods yard closing in 1972 and the signal box and most of the remaining sidings taken out of use in 1987.

The present day Weymouth station is nothing like its predecessor in terms of traffic or overall size; the current building is a relatively modern structure, having been rebuilt in 1986 utilising the two excursion platforms from the alterations

With the designated code of two headlamps across the front buffer beam (as well as the rear buffer beam) of one red and one white light during darkness, 7780 shunts carriage stock at Weymouth on 30 March 1961. The pannier tank, dating from 1930, was one of a batch, 7775-7799, built by Armstrong Whitworth. It was withdrawn from service in June 1963. John Eyers, courtesy South Western Circle.

of 1957 and one short new one. There are thus now three platforms today instead of the original six. The extension of third-rail electrification from Bournemouth in 1988 with the current switched on from 10 February and full services commencing on 16 May has given the station much improved services to London Waterloo which even in steam days was the more direct and faster route, although the GWR had the lions share of the boat trains and freight traffic. Services to and from Waterloo in 2012 are operated by South West Trains with a two trains per hour service, one calling at all stations to Southampton and the other operating a limited stop service to Southampton then fast from Winchester to Waterloo. Class 444 Express Desiro Units are in use, complemented by

End of an era as the fireman of Old Oak's 7010 AVONDALE CASTLE walks forward to change the code from class A headlamps to a tail lamp in readiness to run tender first to the engine shed after arriving at Weymouth Junction with the 08.20 Channel Islands Boat Express from Paddington on Saturday 26 September 1959. This was the last day of the boat train service from Paddington. After the locomotive, restaurant car and leading brake have been detached, the train will then be hauled along the tramway to the Quay station by one of the pannier tanks. AVONDALE CASTLE returned to London later in the day at 16.09 from Weymouth Junction (15.45 from the Quay station) with the last up Channel Islands Boat Express to Paddington. The boat trains were transferred to Waterloo from 3 November though in the interim period passengers used the 18.00 from Paddington. J.D. Blackburn, courtesy Brian Jackson.

occasional appearances by Class 450 Suburban Desiro Units.

Trains over the ex-GWR route are operated on a two-hourly basis by First Great Western between Bristol and Weymouth with a return service of approximately eight trains per weekday with three trains on Sundays plus a further two in the summer. Class 158 Units are used supplemented by Class 150s and on occasions by Class 153s. Many of the services call at the smaller stations by request only, although a fine summer weekend can still conjure memories of the once thriving excursion business. During Summer Saturdays only in 2011 to deal with the extra passenger traffic and the lines resurging popularity, an extra service formed of MK2 coaching stock hauled by a Class 67 was operated between Bristol and Weymouth.

Top. After being coaled, watered, turned and prepared at Weymouth shed, 2-6-0 76016 backs into Weymouth station on 24 September 1966. The 2-6-0s had a low axle loading of less than 17 tons, giving them wide route availability. The Southern Region had the largest allocation (37) of this class of locomotive. John Eyers, South Western Circle.

Middle. 76016 has coupled up to the stock of the 16.47 to Bournemouth Central; it was allocated when new in 1953 to Eastleigh (71A) reallocated to Guildford (70C) in June 1966 and withdrawn on 31 September of the same year, just seven days after this photograph was taken. It was scrapped at Cashmore's Newport in 1967. John Eyers, South Western Circle.

Bottom. 35014 NEDERLAND LINE arrives with the 15.23 from Bournemouth Central on 24 September 1966. John Eyers, South Western Circle.

Top. 76016 with the 16.47 to Bournemouth Central again, but earlier in the year, on 29 June 1966. The DMU on the right is working a service to Bristol Temple Meads along the former GWR route via Dorchester West, Yeovil Pen Mill and Westbury. DMUs had began working services between Bristol and Weymouth with the winter timetable in 1959, gradually interspersing with the local Bristol-Weymouth steam services, until replacing them completely. John Eyers, South Western Circle.

Middle. 34032 CAMELFORD reverses from Weymouth station bound for the engine shed after arriving with the 15.06 from Bournemouth Central (12.35 Waterloo) on 24 September 1966. John Eyers, South Western Circle.

Bottom. 34009 LYME REGIS wreathed in steam at Weymouth station prior to departure with the 17.30 to Waterloo on 24 September 1966. From my own experience as a fireman, the fire and steam pressure has to be exactly right when leaving Weymouth as the climb to Bincombe Tunnel starts almost from the end of the platform. The problem was that a locomotive came down off shed with a more or less 'green' fire and the fireman had to get the firebox red-hot with the fire burning through nicely before departure. Even with a banking locomotive pushing hard at the rear of the train it could be a tricky job to reach the top of the incline. John Eyers, South Western Circle.

WEYMOUTH. Pavilion and Pier.

An Edwardian scene where everyone, male and female, young or old seems to be wearing a hat. The Pavilion theatre opened in 1908 with the pier on ground reclaimed from the sea. The 173ft long GWR baggage hall also containing offices and a refreshment room opened in 1889 with rail passenger services starting in August of that year. At the same time the GWR took over the Channel Islands ferry service from the Weymouth & Channel Islands Steam Packet Company. Three new ships were built in 1889 for the GWR services: *Antelope, Gazelle* and *Prince*. The single track on the pier lasted until the 1930s when an additional track was laid, part of a massive redevelopment of the berthing pier. Begun in 1931, it was in use by May 1933, HRH the Prince of Wales officially opening the new development on 13 July of that year. Further developments on the pier occurred in 1961.

Ex-Burry Port & Gwendraeth Valley Railway 0-6-0ST 2194 KIDWELLY awaits permission to proceed along Commercial Road with a freight train for the tramway in 1929. The BP&GVR was absorbed by the GWR on 1 July 1922. KIDWELLY and sister engine CWM MAWR came to Weymouth in 1926. At 32 tons each they were the heaviest locomotives at the time to work along the tramway. 2194 was withdrawn from Weymouth in 1940. Dr Ian C. Allen, transporttreasury.co.uk

Chapter 5
Memories of the Weymouth Harbour Tramway

One of the many delights of Weymouth, which is as true today as in my childhood in the late 1940s, is the beautiful sandy beach. We had travelled down from our home in Frome by train to spend a week in the resort; happy days in company with my parents and brother in an exquisite summer. Buckets and spades, digging away, building sandcastles in the lovely yellow sand; donkey rides, the smell of candy floss and hot tea emerging from the beach huts doing a roaring trade as holidaymakers queued for jugs of hot steaming tea, ice cream or sandwiches. It was certainly a far different era from today, but a better, kinder one in my view, when most holiday-makers went by train or charabanc. Only the rich could afford holidays abroad, but nevertheless a holiday in an English resort when the weather is kind, is still the best there is.

I well recall sitting on the packed beach, looking across to the sea and watching the majestic progress of the ships sailing out of the harbour into Weymouth Bay then turning and heading for the Channel Islands; those I recall with particular fondness include the *St.Helier,* and *St.Julien.* Then, magically, looking across to the pier and seeing a wisp of steam as a locomotive trundled along with a string of carriages to the Quay station. Later in the day we left the beach and headed for the pier, and for the very first time I viewed the tramway close up. What joy for us boys to walk close by to a simmering pannier tank with a train of carriages waiting alongside the quay platform, and maybe daring to reach out and touch it; gleaming rails set into the roadway which you could *actually walk on,* all combined in a heady atmosphere of ozone and steam. All this plus a beautiful harbour full of fishing boats, and pleasure craft offering trips around the bay to Portland Harbour or Lulworth Cove.

It was a short walk along the harbour to the cargo stage which always seemed to be busy on summer days; lots of shouting and activity with lines of wagons awaiting loading with produce that had arrived from the Channel Islands. Cargo ships with names such as *Roebuck* and *Sambur* were unloaded by vast cranes lifting the precious tomatoes and other vegetables from the holds of the ships and onto the cargo stage where the stevedores loaded the contents into the railway wagons. There always seemed to be a pannier tank waiting at the cargo stage to move the wagons about, the loaded wagons marshalled and replaced by empty ones. And then joy of joys, the distinctive sounds of a bell ringing, the steady chuff of a steam locomotive, and the rumbling and squealing of wheel flanges along the tramway as a passenger train approached. Everybody loved the sight of the trains passing along the roadway, pedestrians enjoying their walk along the harbour would stop to view the proceedings, and cars would have to move quickly out of the way. The shunters, as if from a lost age, walked in front of the locomotive with their red flags, stopping traffic at the various road junctions en route. And everybody including myself as a young boy would follow the train winding its way through the streets and under the town bridge. The train travelled literally at walking pace and would often come to a halt when a parked car blocked its path. A crowd of onlookers would gather to see what would happen; the shunters of course were used to this and the offending vehicle would be 'bounced' aside in the time-honoured way. If this was not possible then the police and a tow-truck

The substantial brick-built former GWR goods shed dated from 1894 and contained two tracks; it replaced an earlier wooden goods shed of 1857, sited further to the east. The many wagons and vans reflect the density of traffic that the railway dealt with at that time. Photograph Graham Herbert courtesy Dorset History Centre.

WEYMOUTH TRAMWAY
OS Map 1959 Crown Copyright Reserved

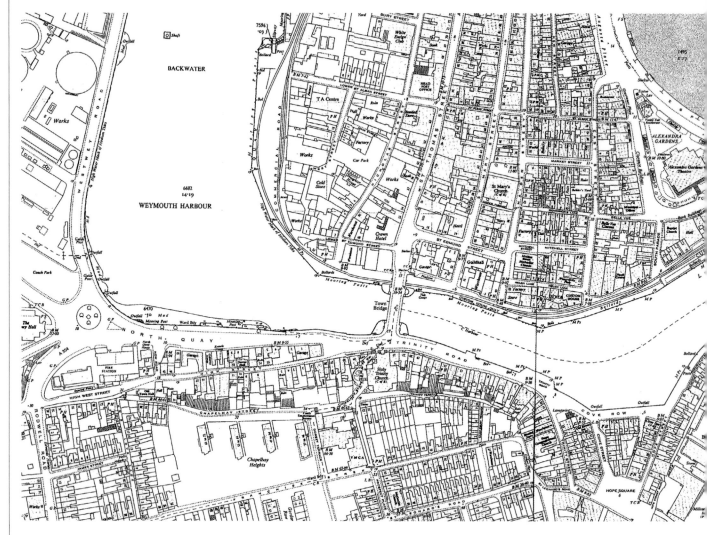

Looking towards Weymouth Junction from the former Easton line on 29 September 1966; the box vans on the right are destined for the cargo stage on the Tramway which was very busy during the summer season with trainloads of flowers, potatoes, cauliflowers and tomatoes arriving from the Channel Islands. The long fully-fitted trains (designated 'Per Pots') conveying produce from the Channel Islands laboured over the gradients of the GWR route to Westbury and beyond with ever increasing frequency, with up to five a day departing from the quay during the 1960s summer season. The Portland branch opened in 1852 and closed to passengers on 3 March 1952 with the remaining goods service withdrawn on 5 April 1965. Track was removed south of Portland in 1966, although the section between Weymouth and the Admiralty sidings remained until 1970. John Eyers, South Western Circle.

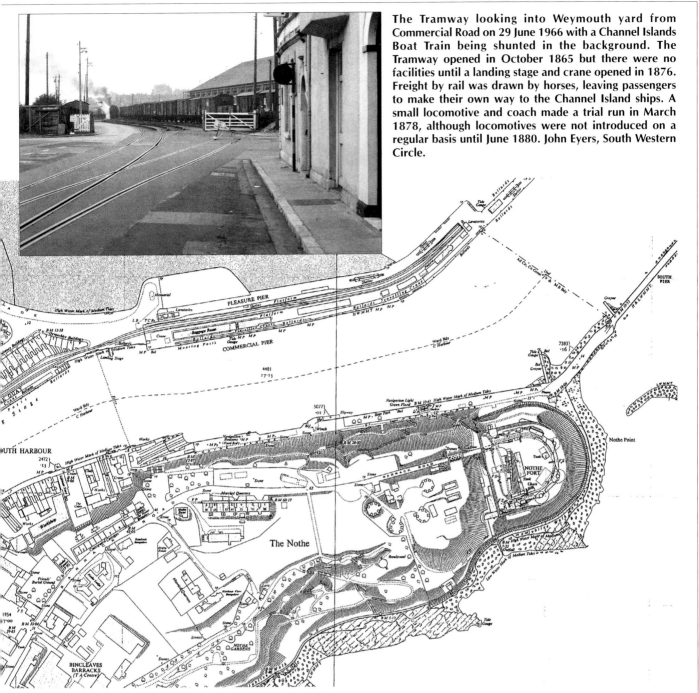

The Tramway looking into Weymouth yard from Commercial Road on 29 June 1966 with a Channel Islands Boat Train being shunted in the background. The Tramway opened in October 1865 but there were no facilities until a landing stage and crane opened in 1876. Freight by rail was drawn by horses, leaving passengers to make their own way to the Channel Island ships. A small locomotive and coach made a trial run in March 1878, although locomotives were not introduced on a regular basis until June 1880. John Eyers, South Western Circle.

Ferry's corner on the Tramway looking in the direction of the Quay station on 29 September 1966. Part of the backwater here was reclaimed and widened in 1938 enabling a track curve of reasonable radius to be laid out. This did away with the time consuming practice (due to the sharp radius of the former curve in use since 1889) of unscrewing the bogie coach couplings and replacing them with three-link loose ones. The links of these replacements were 16 inches long instead of the customary 12 inches and the total length of each loose coupling was some four feet. The only exception was the articulated coaching stock introduced in 1925, but this was only used on the boat trains until about 1934. The new curve seen here on the right now allowed bogie vehicles of up to 70ft to pass without the trouble of re-coupling. The other lines were sidings laid in 1962 to cope with additional freight traffic. John Eyers, South Western Circle.

The exit from Weymouth yard to the Tramway along Commercial Road on 29 September 1966. The final Paddington Channel Islands Boat Express ran on 29 September 1959, the winter service from Waterloo starting on 3 November as the 21.15 to Southampton Docks which was extended to Weymouth on Tuesday and Friday nights. John Eyers, South Western Circle.

The Tramway looking towards the Quay station on 29 September 1966; the cargo stage is on the right past the line of parked vehicles. The track on the far left is the 'main' line of the tramway. From the summer of 1961 with the cessation of sailings from Southampton to the Channel Island all services were transferred to Weymouth, making 'the Tram' busier than ever and up to four boat trains could be seen on a summer Saturday. The trains destined for Waterloo from the Quay station in 1961 departed at 14.45, 1500 and 16.00. The service for Birmingham and Cardiff was scheduled away at 16.15 still using the ex-GWR route via Yeovil and Westbury. John Eyers, South Western Circle.

'Dockie' pannier tank 1367 trundles bunker-first along Commercial Road heading for Weymouth Quay station on 19 September 1955. The tramway was worked without signals or block telegraph and was under the supervision of a tramway inspector handling trains under a time interval system. Speed was limited to 4mph, all locomotives were equipped with a warning bell and a shunter with a red flag walked in front to protect the train at road junctions. A.E.Bennett, transporttreasury.co.uk

Wherever you looked, there was always a clutter of some kind, such as in this illustration of some of the obstacles encountered by trains on the tramway; there were not only parked cars but also stored boats to contend with. A gleaming Mk1 Ford Cortina NGL312 in the foreground is parked carefully away from the rail line, whilst the driver of the Vauxhall Viva APR341B may need a new door if a shunting loco happens to turn up. A boat train can be glimpsed in the background heading towards Weymouth Junction behind a diesel shunter. R.C.Riley, transporttreasury.co.uk

would be called for, leaving the owner with a hefty bill and maybe a fine for blocking the passage of the train, which had right of way over road traffic. The train could be followed as far as the bus garage in Commercial Road whereupon it entered the maze of sidings in Weymouth Yard which was out of bounds to the general public. The tramway was great fun for generations of schoolchildren over the years, placing pennies on the track and in a dare-devil fashion reaching out to touch the steam locomotives and carriages as they rumbled past Happy days, and all in an age when play stations and computers were undreamt of.

History of the Tramway

The Weymouth & Portland Railway Company was incorporated by Act of Parliament on 30 June 1862. Section 16 of the act authorising a *railway or tramway commencing by a junction with the Portland line at or near the junction of that line with the Great Western Railway and terminating at or near the Toll House on the Pile Pier in the Parish of Melcombe Regis.* Construction of the Portland line including the tramway began in December 1862. The first twelve chains of the W&P was on GWR property. The route of the tramway diverged from the Portland line proper and was to be constructed on public roads as far as possible. Both lines were completed by May 1864 but complications with two viaducts on the W&P, and a dispute over station accommodation at Weymouth, meant the opening of the Portland and Tramway lines was delayed until 16 October 1865. The tramway itself was not directly involved with the arguments, but nevertheless as an integral part of the Portland line it had to remain unopened until the difficulties were overcome. The 79 chains of mixed-gauge tramway were single except at the terminus where a short siding was provided. Under an agreement of March 1862 the line was managed, maintained and worked by a Joint Committee of the LSWR and the GWR on a perpetual lease, though the LSWR was not involved directly with the day to day operation of the line. To all intents and purposes it was operated by the GWR.

During the early years of operation goods traffic to Portland and the

Up to three locomotives could be seen at work on the line at the same time. Panniers 1369 and 4624 are near the cargo stage on 9 September 1961. Note the firing shovel jammed into the bunker handrail; I have done this more than once on this type of loco to give a bit more room in the cramped cab. C.L.Caddy.

tramway would be worked in one train, made up in order of brake van, Portland traffic and tramway wagons. These were propelled towards the goods yard gate leading to the tramway; the wagons for the tramway would be uncoupled and taken along the line by horses, whilst the locomotive would run round and travel onwards to Portland. With the quay line open only to freight traffic, passengers bound for the Channel Islands had to make their own way to the pier although the GWR did provide horse-drawn buses. The gauge conversion of the GWR Weymouth route in June 1874, from broad to standard, proved to be a major boost to the port especially for the potato traffic, generating special trains to the Midlands and the north of England. By this time the quay was described as 'narrow and inadequate to cope with existing traffic' and a new wooden landing stage 200ft x 22ft complete with a steam crane was brought into use in 1877. Ever increasing traffic brought forward the case for using locomotives on the quay line and on Tuesday 19 March 1878, the GWR duly obliged. A small locomotive and composite coach were produced for a trial run in order that the Mayor and members of the Corporation could be afforded the opportunity of inspecting one of the small locomotives which it (the GWR) proposed to use on the line. Approval for locomotives to be used was given by members of the Corporation at its next meeting. However, two years were to elapse before a locomotive was actually in regular service, from Monday 7 June

1880 for the hauling of wagons between the station and the tramway. Horses were still used for minor shunting and indeed were still mentioned in the operating instructions as late as 1931.

From 1880, too, the tramway was worked independently, rather than as part of the Portland line. With locomotives special regulations were brought into force in the same year, restricting speed to four miles per hour or slower. The engine had always to be accompanied by a 'Policeman in uniform' who was armed with 'a Guards Whistle and a red flag by day and a Guards hand lamp by night.' He was also responsible for seeing that the roadway in front of the engine was clear. The regulations lasted until the end of services on the tramway although in later years the term 'shunter' would replace Policeman. An agreement of 15 August 1888 between the GWR and Weymouth Corporation required the Corporation for its part *to dredge the harbour as required, maintaining a minimum depth of twelve feet, to purchase and demolish properties on the south side of the harbour opposite the custom house to permit swinging of ships, to erect a landing stage with all necessary passenger accommodation including a rail platform and direct rail access*, all to be complete by 30 June 1899. The GWR agreed 'on or before 1 July 1899' *to improve steamer services* [to the Channel Islands] *and to maintain it at least bi-weekly with steamers of minimum specified tonnage, also in the event of transferring services to Portland to pay the*

cost of the work in proportion. The GWR was empowered to increase the clearance under the town bridge arch to permit the passage of carriage stock over the tramway and to extend the tram-way as necessary at the company's own expense. The archway was duly raised to a height of 13ft 6ins and widened to 14ft; an eight-wheeled bogie coach was attached to the tramway engine and hauled from the station to the quay to test for clearances on 20 June 1899.

Pannier tank 1370 at the Quay station on 24 July 1958, a view showing the extra track and platform on the left dating from the 1931-33 improvements and the limited space available to install a third track plus an island platform for the future 1961 improvements. In order to squeeze the third track in, the pier platform on the right was cut back by six feet, allowing the existing Nos.1 and 2 roads to be slewed over and the original 1889 pier platform to be raised. The new island platform, at 10ft wide, was 2ft narrower than the back-road platform (on the left in this view) it replaced. The steamship *St. Helier* of 1925 was requisitioned as a troop ship during the Second World War, taking part in the evacuation from Dunkirk; as HMS *St. Helier* it landed Canadian troops at Normandy in 1944. After the war the ship returned to the GWR and resumed the nightly Weymouth-Channel Islands service in 1946; upon nationalisation in 1948 the ship became part of the British Transport Commission fleet. R.C.Riley, transporttreasury.co.uk

A new landing stage of 1899 consisted of a wooden deck 200ft long x 50ft wide supported on cast iron pillars, complete with a 173ft baggage hall including offices and a refreshment room. The tramway was extended by 475ft with the final 220ft on the pier itself. A maximum of four bogie coaches could now be accommodated alongside the landing stage but passengers had to descend from the train using wooden portable steps. Passenger services over the tramway commenced in August of the same year and at the same time the GWR took over working the service to the Channel Islands from the ailing Weymouth and Channel Islands Steam Packet Company. Three brand new ships, *Antelope*, *Gazelle* and *Lynx* were built in 1889 at a cost of £25,000 each by Laird Brothers of Birkenhead for the GWR Weymouth-Channel Islands services. Coal for the ships was transferred from wagons to barges using a siding at the west end of the cargo stage. Further improvements came to Weymouth Pier on 21 December 1908 when the Pavilion Theatre was opened on reclaimed land at the southern end of the esplanade.

During the 1930s ever increasing demands on the passenger and freight services meant that redevelopment of the pier and tramway was sorely needed. By far the most notable improvements were started in 1931, culminating in 1933 when the Prince of Wales officially opened the new works on 13 July. At a cost of over £150,000 the new reinforced concrete

berthing pier now had a total length of 1,300ft. Varying in width from100ft at the southern end to 40ft at the sea end it was capable of handling one passenger vessel, three cargo and two pleasure steamers. The terminus was enlarged to two platforms doing away with the need for portable wooden steps; track in the station area was doubled with each able to hold a full length passenger train or approximately fifty goods wagons. Five electric cranes, electrically operated capstans (never used) and other modern equipment was provided. Facilities for passengers included a new refreshment room and other improvements; it all came into use from May 1933, prior to the official opening, when a Saturday Birmingham train was diverted from the Town station to the quay.

During 1938/39 the roadway was widened at Ferry's Corner, thus doing away with the time consuming use of special 48 inch three link loose couplings. Before this, bogie coaches had only been able to negotiate the corner with their screw-couplings disconnected and replaced by the loose couplings, gangways disconnected and vestibule doors locked.

The tramway was of course out of use during the Second World War and services only resumed on 18 September 1945. The wooden cargo stage dating from the 1870s was reconstructed in 1951 and an extra platform was provided at the quay station in 1961 to deal with the extra traffic resulting from the cessation of sailings to the Channel Islands from

Southampton. Alterations were made in 1980 for the provision of car ferry services to St Malo and the Channel Islands. Services from Weymouth to the Channel Islands and St. Malo in 2012 were transferred to run from Poole due to a defect in the quay wall at Weymouth; hopefully this is only a temporary measure.

Boat trains from Paddington ceased at the end of the summer service on 26 September 1959 and switched to the Waterloo route from 3 November. The last regular scheduled service along the tramway ran on 26 September 1987; there have since been a number of enthusiast specials but the last ran in 1999. Goods services ceased in 1972 except for fuel oil trains, which continued until 1983.The track is still extant but unused, and in January 2009 it was reported that the Weymouth & Portland Borough Council wished to remove the remnants. With Network Rail having no interest in its retention, the council agreed to purchase the line for £50,000 in February of the same year, prior to making a final decision on its future. The status of the tramway is unusual and complex, and involves the Weymouth & Portland Borough Council as owner of the freehold, Network Rail which owns the railway assets and the rights to operate trains and Dorset County Council as the highway authority. The present condition of the tramway is such that considerable work would be required to bring it up to operational standards, while modern

There would always be onlookers at the pier station especially when a ship had arrived from the Channel Islands. A railway porter pushes his barrow across the tracks taking passenger luggage to cars or taxis; more people are walking along the platform with their cases. An 0-6-0 diesel stands alongside platform 1 waiting to haul the boat train to Weymouth Junction and 0-6-0PT 9620 is alongside the island platform on No.2 road. The new island platform and additional third track date from the improvements of 1961; all Channel Islands services were based at Weymouth from the summer of that year. The 1899 GWR baggage hall survived until a new two-storey passenger terminal opened in June 1963. transporttreasury.co.uk

Looking towards the end of the pier from a train standing on No.1 road; No.2 road is in the centre with No.3 on the left. The pre-cast component sections of the 1961 platform including the supporting struts are seen to good effect. The wheeled tank wagon was used to fill the roof top carriage water tanks for toilets and hand basins etc. transporttreasury.co.uk

The photographer has now turned his camera around and is looking towards the station exit. The very narrow 10ft wide pre-cast concrete island platform 2 and 3 on the right dates from 1961. There is an interesting selection of parcels vans along platform 3. The building rising above the rail vans is the Pavilion Theatre opened in 1960 after fire destroyed the building of 1908. transporttreasury.co.uk

notions of risk render any thought of operation prohibitively expensive. A number of speculative and imaginary ideas for trams and suchlike have arisen over the years but costs and feasibility make the likelihood of any reinstatement extremely remote.

In view of the historical significance of the tramway, and as part of the development brief for the Pavilion/Ferry Terminal the Council have set out a proposed conservation strategy which involves preserving sections where it is safe to do so; indeed this has already occurred, in the creation of the Harbourside Walkway at the loop. Block paving set flush into the carriageway could possibly mark the route, and interpretation boards could explain the history of the tramway.

Whilst the scheme for the Pavilion/Ferry Terminal area does not propose building on the tramway sidings area, it does envisage the use of the area for the new Ferry Terminal and its waiting areas, significant level changes and the removal of the former Weymouth Pier Station building which is suffering from subsidence. Whatever happens, it is very doubtful indeed that trains will ever be seen running along the tramway again.

Looking towards the end of the pier with a couple of wagons stabled at the head-shunt. The two-storey buildings were part of the improvements of 1961, replacing single-storey buildings on the pier in order to develop more space for the mechanised handling of freight. The Austin FG lorry does not have a registration plate and so may be a brand new vehicle awaiting export to one of the Channel Islands. If so it will be hoisted by an electric crane (one of which is standing in front of the lorry) and lowered into the hold of a ship moored alongside the pier. Presumably the suitcase in the foreground belongs to the photographer; an item left like this unattended in 2012 will definitely cause a security alert. transporttreasury.co.uk

St. Patrick, flagship of the Weymouth fleet with the GWR coat of arms displayed proudly on her bow, moored alongside the pier at Weymouth. Built in 1947 for the GWR she made her maiden voyage from Weymouth to the Channel Islands on 4 February 1948. The third GWR ship to bear the name, her forebear was sunk on Friday 13 July 1941 by German aircraft off Fishguard with the loss of thirty passengers and crew including her Captain. A diesel shunter has the boat train on track 1. Motor vehicles of the era include a Vauxhall Cresta on the far left, with an Isetta bubble-car sandwiched between a Ford car and an Austin FG lorry RJT 259 belonging to the Weymouth company of Cosens and Co Ltd, well known for their impressive fleet of paddle steamers. transporttreasury.co.uk

The photographer's suitcase seems likely to trip the unwary in this view taken on the pier platform at Weymouth. Two ships are moored alongside and carriage doors on Set 277 standing on track 1 are open awaiting passengers. Freight and mailbags waiting to be loaded on ship or train stretch as far as the eye can see. The majestic electric cranes dating from the major development of the pier in 1933 were always a landmark from the beach with their tall jibs (five jibs can be seen in this photograph) dipping, raising and swinging as ships were unloaded and loaded.
transporttreasury.co.uk

The harbour at Weymouth still is one of the most picturesque in the West of England as seen here in this summer view with pleasure craft and yachts moored line abreast in twos and threes. The driver of the Bedford lorry in the foreground seems to have parked his vehicle rather close to the tramway and will have to move out of the way if a train comes along. transporttreasury.co.uk

A Bulleid Pacific approaches Bincombe Tunnel signal box on the down main line. The box was situated at the north end of Bincombe Tunnel at the summit of the four mile ascent from Weymouth at a gradient of 1 in 52. The engine siding between the main lines stabled the banking locomotives awaiting a path back to Weymouth for which a journey time of ten minutes was allowed. A.Marriott, transporttreasury.co.uk

Chapter 6
Banking on the Weymouth Line
THE EVERSHOT AND UPWEY BANKING LOCOMOTIVES

Yetminster station, 4¾ miles south-east of Yeovil on the ex-GWR Weymouth main line, lies at the bottom of a formidable incline ascending at about 1 in 51 for 5½ miles to Evershot station at the summit. As well as the ascent, which was bad enough for steam crews working Weymouth-bound services, there was also a reverse curve almost half-way which itself could give problems especially with freight trains, as the wheels of the wagons would bind against the rail. Then there was the weather; high winds blowing against the sides of vans would effectively add extra weight. All of this, plus Holywell Tunnel and a set of catch-points at the steepest part of the climb made this a severe test for footplatemen, especially if they were already having a rough trip.

When I was a fireman, Yeovil Town shed supplied the locomotives used for Evershot banking, though prior to closure in 1959 the ex-GWR (by then ex-WR too) shed at Yeovil Pen Mill had provided the locomotives and crews. Although as Southern Region men we worked the Evershot bankers as part of the Town shed diagrams, there was no provision for banking locomotives on our main line

between Salisbury and Exeter Central; in fact the only banking locomotives to be found were on the incline between Exeter St David's and Central stations. As for the rest of the SR main line west of Salisbury, steam locomotives and their crews had to contend unassisted with inclines at Sherborne, Gillingham, Chard Junction and, the worst of them all, the climb from Seaton Junction to the summit at Honiton Tunnel. In common with crews from Yeovil Town and Exmouth Junction I have made this trip in all kinds of weather, struggling at times reach the top; no bankers for us Southern men – we just got on with it!

During the week, and especially during the winter months, the station pilot at Yeovil Pen Mill, which would normally be a pannier or prairie tank working double or treble shifts, would suffice for banking and would assist a train direct from Pen Mill, coupling to the rear of the Weymouth-bound train, either passenger or freight. When banking trains from Yetminster we would not couple up, and upon reaching Evershot station, 500 feet above sea-level, we would cease pushing and the train would proceed onwards to Weymouth running down the bank to

Maiden Newton; at times the train engine would give a toot on the whistle as a thank you. If we banked from Yeovil Pen Mill the train, either freight or passenger, would came to a halt in Evershot station in order for the assisting locomotive to uncouple and let the train set off on its journey. As for the banker the signalman would switch the loco over to the up main line and after refilling with water from the column off the end of the up platform would return to Yetminster; if it was the end of a shift we'd return light engine to Yeovil Pen Mill for which a time of 22 minutes was allotted. All unfitted up freight trains stopped at Evershot to pin down brakes for the descent to Yetminster. During the hours when Evershot signal box was switched out we would go as far as Maiden Newton before returning back to Yeovil via the up main line. We would stop pushing at Evershot and just trundle from there onwards at the rear of the train on the descent to Maiden Newton, letting the engine at the front do all the braking.

At other times the station pilot would be despatched to Yetminster light engine to await the train that required assistance. The everyday Bristol to

The first signal box at Bincombe opened in 1876 and was replaced by this 13 lever box in 1896. The engine siding was also brought into use at the same time and lasted until September 1969 before it was abandoned. The signal box survived until closure on 1 March 1970 with the engine siding removed on 4 October of the same year. The down main line was slewed over the site of the former siding in December 1980. A.Marriott, transporttreasury.co.uk

Top. **Lord Nelson 4-6-0 30864 SIR MARTIN FROBISHER runs downhill from Bincombe North tunnel with a Bournemouth to Weymouth service on 31 May 1950. Underneath the grime the locomotive is in 1948 experimental Apple Green livery. The wooden arm lower quadrant signal on the left with a distinctive lean is the Bincombe Tunnel signal box up distant. J.C.Flemons, transporttreasury.co.uk**

Above. **St Philips Marsh 2-6-0 5323 runs cautiously downhill out of Bincombe North tunnel with a Bristol-Weymouth freight on 10 July 1956. R.C.Riley, transporttreasury.co.uk**

Weymouth passenger services would not normally request assistance as they were often under the maximum loading for the bank although they were entitled to request the banker if the locomotive was not steaming too well. The heaviest trains that needed a push up the bank included the Bristol East Depot and Severn Tunnel Junction freights, which needed a fair amount of shoving to get them up to the top. Freights were hauled by a variety of locomotive types including 28XX, 43XX, Stanier Black Fives, WD 2-8-0s, Standard Class 5MTs and I have known a 9F 2-10-0 to arrive on occasions.

Like all of my former colleagues from Yeovil Town shed I have had my share of shunting in the down sidings at Yeovil Pen Mill. This was a busy yard dealing mainly with transfer freight which was tripped to Hendford Goods on the Western side of Yeovil; freight was also despatched to Yeovil Junction, all of it going via Yeovil

Town. Most firemen could find shunting tedious, as there were spells of activity combined with long periods of standing stationary. The fireman had little to do except keep the fire banked up under the firehole door; not enough to create excess steam, but enough to push forward if we were told to bank a Weymouth train. On one particular day I was booked on the Pen Mill station pilot with a U Class 2-6-0 and after a break in shunting duties it was time for a cup of tea and a bite to eat. At that time the station had a bookstall on the up platform and I usually took the chance to nip over and buy a newspaper to while away the time. It was always welcome to be informed that a particular train required a banker, for this meant that we could escape the yard and take to the main line.

A Bristol-Weymouth freight duly arrived behind a grimy and unkempt Stanier Black Five leaking steam from

every pipe and joint. It groaned to a stop alongside the water column by the down platform, definitely the worse for steam, judging by the hiss of the steam blower from the chimney. Black Fives had a good reputation for steaming, but as was the case in steam days, rarely were two engines from the same class alike for steaming and riding. After refilling the tender and dropping off to collect wagons from the yard it had returned to the head of the train, the Pen Mill starting and South Junction distant signal arms were lowered, and we were ready to go. By this time we had been released from the yard at its eastern end and were already coupled to the brake van, from which the Guard had already removed the tail lamps as our tail lamp on the tender would indicate the rear of the train in accordance with regulations for the journey to Evershot.

I had already levelled our fire with the long handled pricker and the firebox was now red-hot, steam pressure was rising, the footplate was all washed down and the coal in the tender had had a good soaking for good measure. As always we were awaiting the whistle call from the train locomotive; it soon came, the deep note of the Stanier hooter reverberated around the station, my mate already had our whistle cord in his hand, and our reply also echoed around the station. We started pushing as soon as the brake van started to move, my mate wound back the reverser and had the regulator just cracked open and our water gauge glasses had approximately three quarters of a glass; just right, and time to close the firebox doors. Now gathering speed as we passed under the A30 road bridge, approaching Yeovil South Junction the long train of wagons rumbled around the curve and past the junction with the wartime signal box and the tracks connecting Yeovil Town with Yeovil Junction. We were going well as we passed underneath the Salisbury-Exeter main line at Clifton Maybank and my mate had not yet given our locomotive full regulator; this would not happen until the Yetminster distant signal was seen to be off. A black exhaust from the Black Five at the head of the train showed that the fireman was tending to his fire. On our footplate the steam pressure was good, and the firebox under control with a box of red-hot fire; no need to put on coal yet, but the time for it was approaching. The lowered arm of the Yetminster distant signal soon came into view and now was the time for full regulator as we sailed past the station and our speed dramatically decreased as we hit into the bank. Our engine was now barking away, as I tended to the needs of the firebox, shovelling coal where it was required, mostly under the firedoor and the back corners. The injector was on and singing away as I topped up the boiler and washed down the footplate and tender at the same time to keep the dust down.

The train engine in front was throwing out vast clouds of smoke and exhaust steam and we were doing exactly the same; however the Black Five was not doing too well and our progress slowed even further, every piece of our locomotive now straining with power and the exhaust was deafening. The firebox was now white hot as I fed it with coal, at the same time keeping an eye on the water and steam gauges. We were now working on full regulator and three quarter cut off on the reverser, and if we had any chance to get this train to the top of the bank, then we had to give our all. My mate spun the reverser into full forward gear and the response from our chimney was dramatic and our exhaust, already deafening, was now ear splitting. The beat on the fire was tremendous, and the heat from the firebox when I opened the firedoors took the breath from my lungs.

As we gratefully neared the top of the bank with the lowered arm of Evershot's distant signal coming into view complete with its set of catch points, the gaping mouth of the 308 yard long Holywell Tunnel also appeared with the smoke and steam from the Black Five already issuing from it. As we entered the dark of the tunnel it was lit up with the reflection of our firebox, and it was a job to breathe the smoke and steam-laden air. Our exhaust pounded against the roof, showering red hot cinders and char everywhere; you could hardly see your hands in front of your face.

Our exhaust beat muffled as we left the tunnel over the last few yards of the bank and coasted into Evershot station where we came to a halt. The guard would uncouple us from his brake van and replace his tail lamps. After a short interval the freight train departed for Weymouth, the signalman crossed us over to the up main line and, after refilling

our tender with water at the end of the platform, we departed tender-first for Yeovil. At the peak weekends during the summer service, two or even three banking locomotives would be standing on the siding by the signalbox at Yetminster Working on the bankers involved periods of inactivity coupled with frantic bursts of activity as you struggled to push a train up over the ascent to Evershot.

Summer Saturdays in the 1950s would bring many extra services including four Saturday Channel Islands Boat Trains which would be overloaded for the bank and therefore require assistance. Trains that needed banking included:
08.20 and 08.30 ex-Paddington booked to pass Pen Mill at 11.00 and 11.16 respectively
07.50 and 08.00 ex-Birmingham
08.30 ex-Weston-Super-Mare
09.10 ex-Bristol
09.34 ex-Reading General
12.30 ex-Paddington
11.05 ex-Wolverhampton
21.00 ex-Paddington.

Busy weekends and bank holidays would also bring extra excursion traffic, which needed banking. All of the ex-GWR named passenger classes, with the exception of the Kings, would be found on the Weymouth services. Banking took place all the year round, and when Evershot signal box was switched out at night, the banking engines would continue to Maiden Newton and return from there to Pen Mill.

I have many memories, good and not so good, regarding the banking duties, and

one of the worst took place one winter night, in dense fog when the brake van in front of our engine was more or less invisible. A wonderful time would be a summer evening after banking the 21.30 Paddington-Weymouth Quay boat train, and coasting down the bank returning to Yeovil Town shed on one of our prairie tanks, 5548 with Driver Fred Symonds. Both of us contentedly leaning over our respective cabside puffing on our cigarettes; firedoors open with the glow of the fire reflecting around the inside of the cab, every star in the sky twinkling and glowing, and the sound of our engine piston valves as we ran light engine was just perfect. Happy Days and nights on the bankers at Evershot.

****

The four-mile ascent from Weymouth at 1 in 52, culminating in the notorious 814 yard Bincombe Tunnel at the north end, is a severe test. In 2012 diesel and electric trains glide effortlessly up the incline, but back in steam days it was a far different story; most, but not quite all of the steam services departing from Weymouth were assisted on their way to the summit by banking locomotives and their crews from Weymouth shed. In fact Isambard Kingdom Brunel had put forward the suggestion in 1844 that the Wilts, Somerset & Weymouth with its gradient problems should be worked on the (as it turned out ill-fated) 'Atmospheric' system. Captain Moorsom, engineer to the Southampton & Dorchester Railway, also favoured using it between Weymouth and Dorchester but the idea fortunately did not come to fruition.

5323 with safety valves lifting and running under light steam with the driver braking and keeping the train in check to avoid a runaway, descends towards Upwey & Broadway with that Bristol-Weymouth freight on 10 July 1956. R.C.Riley, transporttreasury.co.uk

The brick-built coal stage at Weymouth shed in 1957. The ramp was on an incline of approx. 1 in 35, levelling off for about 100ft beyond the stage on the left where the loaded wagons were stabled. Staff messrooms were provided at ground level. A.E.West, courtesy Mike King.

Trains would leave Weymouth station and come to a halt adjacent to Jubilee Sidings to await the banker, which would come to the rear of the train and push uncoupled as far as Bincombe Signal box north of the tunnel. Here the banker would drop off and enter the double-ended siding to return to Weymouth, for which ten minutes running time was allowed. They might find another up train waiting at Upwey and Broadwey for assistance; this would mean a harder task for the banker crew as the train would be at a standstill halfway up the bank, with no chance of 'a run at it'. Boat trains arriving from the quay would be assisted once the main line engine had replaced the tramway locomotive. When working the return excursion trains back to Yeovil Pen Mill from Weymouth for instance, passing Jubilee Sidings was the time to request a banker or not. The recognised sign from the banking engine driver was to make a fist of one hand pushed into the palm of the other; this meant 'do you want a banker?' and in my time the reply was always 'No' as we usually had one of our superb U Class 2-6-0s or (on one occasion) a Bulleid Pacific to get us home.

B ill Waters, former Weymouth footplateman, recalls his experiences: 'In the 1960s I was working as a passed engine cleaner/fireman at Weymouth engine shed. I was booked on duty one Saturday as the late-turn shed fireman from 14.00 to 22.00 with an "old hand driver" and we spent the time moving engines from the fire-dropping pit and coal stage to the turntable to turn the locos for their next duty. The turntable at Weymouth was hand-powered, so the engine had to be stopped at the point of balance or it could not be moved. The day was going well, moving locos into the shed roads and shunting them alongside the coal stage; for a 16 year old the shed turn was a good job as the drivers did not like continually getting on and off the engines, this meant that the fireman did most of the driving on the shed duties.

'At about 20.30 the driver said to me "Bill, turn the last engine to arrive on

shed tonight would you, I'm going down to the club, it will only be a 76". At 21.15 the engine turned up, only it was Merchant Navy Pacific 35030 ELDER DEMPSTER LINES and not a 76000 2-6-0. The engine was on the fire dropping pit when Scobie, the fire dropper, handed it over to me; with the assistance of an engine cleaner I moved the Pacific, now very low in steam, on to the table. The cleaner asked me to move it forward as it was not balanced. I placed the engine in forward gear and opened the regulator, but because of the low steam pressure it would not move. So I closed the cylinder cocks and opened the regulator again, this time the engine moved, and as it came into balance the turntable moved about two feet and the cleaner called out for me to stop.

'I closed the regulator and put the vacuum brake on but she kept moving! ELDER DEMPSTER LINES nose-dived and stopped with the cab pointing towards the full moon. The cleaner optimistically suggested that we get steam up and drive it back on, but I thought not: "No, we'd better tell the running foreman." We trudged into his office and told him that we were off the road at the turntable. He looked at us and said, "Stop messing about and go home!" or something similar. "No Les I replied "WE'RE OFF THE ROAD!"

'We all left the shed heading for the turntable. Les looked at the engine: "S—T where's the driver? I explained that he was at the club and was immediately sent off to fetch him. With the driver (somewhat put out) back from the club and with the assistance of the night shift fitters we uncoupled the tender moving it off the table onto some sleepers; the engine was jacked up and sleepers placed under the rear wheels, steam was raised and the engine moved back onto the turntable. With the tender re-coupled it was turned and placed in the shed.

'The following morning I was standing in front of Mr Blackman the Shed Master, "DO NOT DO IT AGAIN WILLIAM" was all he said.

'One day in the 1960s a young fireman was preparing his engine, a Class 5 Standard 4-6-0. Filling the tender from a column outside the running shed, his driver told him "When you've finished, take the engine over for coal, I'm going to see the running foreman". Now it should be pointed out that in order to stop the bag on the column moving away from the tender during watering it was common practice to wrap the chain around the

During a respite from normal duties on the tramway 1366 class 0-6-0PT 1370 shunts coal wagons at Weymouth shed in 1957. Any spare engine would be used for this job and with much slipping and sliding on greasy or wet rails loaded wagons would be propelled up the incline to the coal stage. Note the bell on the engine framing which was obligatory for locomotives working on the tramway. A.E.West, courtesy Mike King.

handrail on the top of the tender. Having turned off the water, the fireman, forgetting to remove the chain, set off for the coal stage, readers will now be aware that the loco has started to move whilst the water column chain is still attached to the tender hand-rail, and will be wondering what the outcome will be, will the chain break?

'You'd think so but no... the water column *comes out of the ground* and the six-inch pipe breaks off on the wrong side of the stop valve. We are left with a fountain of water 30ft high, flooding to the tops of the rails, but no water for the locomotives.

'Weymouth shed had a coal bank with an incline of approximately 1 in 14 to get coal wagons to the top of the stage; here they would be unloaded into small 4-wheeled iron tubs. The tubs would then be moved out on rails, above the waiting locomotives and tipped into the tender or bunker. To shunt the coal bank, the shed driver and fireman would take a spare engine and move towards the exit road stop; the fireman would place the semaphore signal to danger to prevent locos coming off shed while the coal bank was being shunted. To stop any runaway wagons from reaching Weymouth station the coal bank had a spring catch point to derail them. The fireman would go and stand on the treadle of the spring point whilst the driver moved the engine to the top of the bank to collect the empty wagons and remove them to the loco yard, then collect five loaded wagons of coal and set back onto the engine release line to Weymouth station from where he would take a run at the bank.

'On this particular day the engine, a 41XX class 2-6-2T, was pushing its loaded coal wagons hard to get to the summit of the bank, past the fireman standing on the spring point, in time-honoured fashion. Just then a 73000 BR Standard 4-6-0 whistled up for permission to pass the shed signal. At that moment, the loco on the coal bank didn't quite make the summit and the loaded coal wagons started to push it back down the slope. The fireman, not wishing to derail his driver, stayed where he was holding the spring-point. The driver of the '73' Standard seeing the 41 tank slipping and in difficulties, opened his regulator in order to get out of the way, but to no avail. As the Standard slipped on the pointwork, the tank loco collided with it, knocking it over about 45 degrees. All the wheels of the tank loco ended up off the road with the five wagons piled up on top of one another.

'One of my first firing turns at Weymouth was on the second passenger yard pilot. We spent the duty taking empty coaching stock from Weymouth station and stabling the stock in the Jubilee sidings. Our engine that day was an Ivatt 2-6-2T, 41305. At the end of our shift we were asked to bank a train up to Bincombe and for my first firing turn I thought this was great. And in fact in my time at Weymouth I did a lot of work on the banking turns. When working on the banker, if the train was going to stop at Dorchester the assisting engine had to be coupled to the front with the main locomotive, but if it was a boat train or goods train the banker would buffer up uncoupled at the rear of the train and assist as far as Bincombe Tunnel signal box, once there we would use the crossover and return to Weymouth light engine.

'There was a middle siding at Bincombe, where in busy times we would wait for our return path, so if a following train complete with banker was coming up the bank, that engine would couple up to us upon arrival after assisting his train, and we would return to Weymouth in one move. When working on the bankers at night, you would be displaying a white headlamp on the front and red to the rear; during daylight the lamps would not be lit.

'I had a bad blowback when working the banking turn one day. We had returned to shed at about 14.00 for a tea break after assisting trains up the bank. Whilst sitting in the drivers cabin the running foreman came in and told us that we would have to bank one more train before the end of our duty. I went out into the shed yard, climbed aboard our locomotive and looked into the firebox; the fire was black with small blue flames on the top of the coal and a haze in the roof of the firebox. I took out the pricker to stir and liven the fire.

'It livened up alright! There was an almighty bang, flames shot out of the firebox door and the locomotive shook, frightening the life out of me. My driver asked if I was OK and I thought I was. No time to recover of course, so we set off from the shed to bank one more train.

'I had a rough trip up the bank with a rebuilt West Country, a full load on and no banker. We set off from Weymouth, doing well until we reached Bincombe Tunnel; about half-way through, the Pacific slipped, and such was the noise and smoke, we didn't know if we were moving forwards or slipping back. We were grimly aware of the trap point just outside the tunnel to derail any runaway. The recourse was to grab the firing shovel, lean out of the cab and touch the tunnel wall with it, this would reveal what was going on. Fortunately we were inching forward and after what seemed ages we managed to clear the tunnel and reach the top of the incline.

'One day I was on a 73000 4-6-0 in a siding waiting to bank a boat train at the Weymouth end of the yard near where the tramway enters the yard from the quay. I was on the footplate age 16 years old and not wearing my overall jacket and the driver had wandered off somewhere. At that time a public footpath crossed over the Portland branch, the sidings and the end of the tramway. Some holidaymakers came walking along the path and the man in the group shouted out "Son what are you doing on that engine, get off at once" he was about 45 years old – ancient! I protested that I was the fireman, but he didn't believe me. "You can't be! I'm a fireman and you look like a schoolboy". With that my driver climbed aboard; the boat train had turned up, and so we set off to assist him as far as Bincombe.

'The tramway was good fun. We were shunting in Weymouth yard and when my driver went for a walk I carried on with the driving in his absence. There was a break from shunting and I went to have a cup of tea in the shunters cabin at Weymouth Junction. The yard foreman came in and told me I would have to take the train down to the quay straightaway. "What about the driver?" I protested. The shunter opined that as I had been driving the loco up and down the yard for the last hour or so, then I could take the train along to the quay. This would be the first time that I had driven a locomotive and seven coaches to the quay! So I set off with the train rumbling along behind the locomotive but had only been on Commercial Road for a short distance when my driver, Ed Trivett climbed aboard near the Westham Road junction, sat on the fireman's seat and proceeded to read a newspaper. Some 40 years later I was the mobile operations manager at Yeovil Junction. I received a telephone message from a driver at Euston to say that he had seen a photo of me driving on the tramway and no sign of a driver! I think it's a bit too late to report it now.

'At one time on the quay, apples were being imported to be made into cider, and in order to move this traffic the railway used empty 16 ton coal wagons. An attempt had been made to clean them out, but they still carried a fair amount of coal dust which no doubt added to the flavour of the cider. The wagons were worked along the tramway and into the loop, the locomotive would stay on the front and as each wagon was loaded with apples by a crane fitted with a grab, the loco would move forward for the next to be loaded. The only trouble was that the apples, being round as apples are, and stacked high on the wagons, the top layer would roll off on to the roadway and then between the rail flanges. As the trains worked up and down the tramway the apples turned into pulp and our locomotive would spend the rest of the day slipping and sliding. After a time it proved awkward not only to get the train moving but also to make it stop, and all this on a public road.

'One day at the Quay station we were going to tail a boat train and were in the loop when the train passed us. With me, the driver and two shunters in the cab we set back over the points which were all spring-loaded on the tramway and set for the main line. The driver moved forward and with no one looking at the points we became derailed with all six wheels. I asked my driver should I telephone the shed, he said no and placed the engine into reverse and opened the regulator, we lurched back onto the track leaving a set of wheel marks in the tarmac.

'One day down at the quay a fisherman just prior to us leaving with a boat train gave us some mackerel. Instead of storing them in the cab, I hung them over the outside handrail of our locomotive. Imagine my surprise some 25 years later when the picture of our locomotive complete with the mackerel appeared in a steam enthusiast magazine.

Weymouth Bay and the beach gently curving round to the harbour in the distance; the building on the waters edge in the foreground is the Pier Bandstand. Graham Herbert, courtesy Dorset History Centre.

Holiday visitors stroll outside the entrance to the Pier Bandstand, built in the art deco style and opened on 25 May 1939. The billboard on the wall is advertising Ted Heath and his Music. Heath's was the greatest show band of its day and the show would have been well patronised. Well remembered too, is Harry Hudson and his Show Band, 'currently playing' if the sign above the entrance is anything to go by. Graham Herbert, courtesy Dorset History Centre.

Chapter 7
Welcome to Weymouth!
Holidays in the 1950s

One of the great traditions of the English seaside is the Punch and Judy show which thankfully still survives to this day in Weymouth. This view in the 1950s shows children and parents enjoying the show and its peculiar characters including Punch with his squeaky voice, Judy, Joey the clown, the Beadle, the policeman and of course not forgetting the crocodile and the sausages! Graham Herbert, courtesy Dorset History Centre.

The days when a car could be parked all day on the front for free; this is 21 July 1954, with a fine vista of Weymouth Bay and the small fun fair on the beach. Graham Herbert, courtesy Dorset History Centre.

Inside the Pier Bandstand with ladies in one of the popular bathing beauty competitions in 1958. The bandstand in the background was very popular with concerts by the leading musical figures of the day. Graham Herbert, courtesy Dorset History Centre.

A childrens talent contest in full swing at the Pier Bandstand with the Harry Hudson Show Band. Harry went on to play the piano for Wilfred Pickles (replacing Violet Carson who eventually became Ena Sharples in *Coronation Street*) in his 'Have a Go Show' on the BBC. The show ran from 1946 to 1967 and at its peak in the 1950s attracted an audience of 20 million, becoming the most popular variety show on BBC radio. Graham Herbert, courtesy Dorset History Centre.

The childrens talent contest in the Pier Bandstand showing how popular the venue was, especially during the holiday season. I well remember being taken by our parents with my brother in the late 1940s on a lovely warm summer evening to see a musical show here. The place was packed; I can remember a man playing a grand piano but have no idea who it was. Graham Herbert, courtesy Dorset History Centre.

At the end of a long train journey this is what it was all about; burrowing into an English beach, none better than the golden sands at Weymouth. If, *if* the weather is perfect, this is the best entertainment in the world, complete of course with candy floss, toffee apples, ice cream and perhaps a ride on a donkey. Graham Herbert, courtesy Dorset History Centre.

Crazy golf made interesting at last – and there's that pannier tank too... Graham Herbert ,courtesy Dorset History Centre.

There is a fascinating maze of narrow back streets in Weymouth and traffic problems are nothing new; witness the Guy lorry in the livery of Whiteways Wines and a Victory Transport van trying to sort themselves out. A Morris Oxford is parked in front of a Vauxhall by the pavement in the foreground, with a Standard opposite. Foreign cars were a rarity in this era. Graham Herbert, courtesy Dorset History Centre.

The busy junction of St Thomas Street and Westham Road with the man on the motor bike not having much luck with a right turn. A policeman would have to direct the traffic here at times when it became snarled up in the summer. Graham Herbert, courtesy Dorset History Centre.

A great attraction for children and their parents was the miniature railway that ran from Westham Car park along the western side of Radipole Lake. In the summer of 1958 the train is just about to run under the railway bridge that carried the Portland line over the lake and the car park. Chipperfield's Fun Fair is at left with a Scammell 'Showman's' lorry generating electricity. Graham Herbert, courtesy Dorset History Centre.

Weymouth Carnival is held in August slap bang in the middle of the tourist season, a very popular event appreciated by townspeople and visitors alike. Crossing the harbour bridge is a *tableaux* from the Wyke Regis Community Association on a BR lorry. There was no air conditioning on lorries in the 1950s, the driver just opened the windscreen! Graham Herbert, courtesy Dorset History Centre.

King George III frequented the beach at Weymouth during his times of illness, however, it remains a popular destination today for bathing and here two happy campers are making use of the gently sloping beach with its golden sand and shallow water.

The White Ensign flies proudly in the breeze as two Royal Navy Petty Officers and their ladies pose beside HMS *Pellew* moored alongside the quay in Portland Harbour during Navy Day in August 1958. Visitors are having a tour on the deck of the ship. HMS *Pellew* (Pennant Number F62) was a Type 14 anti-submarine frigate of the Blackwood Class. Launched on the River Tyne at Swan Hunter's Shipyard on 29 September 1954, commissioned on 26 July 1956 and broken up at Fleetwood in 1971. As a boy I well remember visiting Portland on a Navy Day when the warships and submarines in the base were open to visitors for the annual three-day event. Photograph Graham Herbert courtesy Dorset History Centre.

All the nice girls love a sailor... HMS *Dundas,* another Blackwood Class anti-submarine Type 14 frigate, at Portland Navy Day in August 1958. Launched on 25 September 1953 at White (Cowes) Shipyard and commissioned on 9 March 1956, she was broken up at Troon in 1983. Unfortunately our politicians in their wisdom decided that this important naval base after its 150-year history had to close; HMS *Argyll*, a Type 23 frigate, was the last Royal Navy ship to sail from the base, on Friday 21 July 1995. The adjoining helicopter station HMS *Osprey* closed in 1999. The former naval base is to be the sailing venue for the 2012 Olympic Games. Photograph Graham Herbert courtesy Dorset History Centre.

Left. The Guinness Festival Clock at the Alexandra Gardens, Weymouth in the summer of 1953; it was the brainchild of Guinness Advertising Manager Martin Pick. The original clock, 25ft high, designed by Lewitt Him and built by clockmakers Baume & Co of Hatton Garden was first exhibited at Battersea Park as part of the Festival of Britain in 1951. Dispelling the gloom of the post-war years the Festival of Britain held on London's South Bank celebrated the Centenary of the 1851 Great Exhibition held in Hyde Park. A similar display of British achievements in science, art, technology and culture was displayed and I well remember as a schoolboy being enthralled by the exhibits at the time. Such was the interest in the clock that many authorities and exhibition promoters requested that Guinness display it at many venues in the UK. Eventually Guinness built eight smaller travelling versions of the clock (of which this is one) which toured the UK for seven years visiting seaside towns, trade fairs, carnivals and department stores. The clock 'performed' every 15 minutes enthralling crowds everywhere with a four and a half minute routine showing the Guinness animals from the famous advertisements created by artist John Gilroy in which the zoo animals made off with the zoo keeper's Guinness! All of the famous animals were in motion for the display, including the sealion, ostrich, pelican, bear, lion, tortoise, kangaroo, crocodile and kinkajou. The zookeeper, a caricature of Gilroy himself also appeared and, of course, the most famous of them all, the Guinness Toucan. Photograph Graham Herbert courtesy Dorset History Centre.

The beach at the southern end of the esplanade is starting to fill on a pleasant summer day with plenty of extra deckchairs stacked in readiness. The extra wide pavement that extends the length of the esplanade has picturesque Victorian cast-iron pagodas to seat the weary or shelter walkers from the sunshine (or rain). Beyond are the jibs of the cranes at the quay, rising, lowering or swinging like some giant's mechanical ballet as ships were loaded and unloaded. Photograph Graham Herbert courtesy Dorset History Centre.

In the 1950s nearly the lorries on the road were made in Great Britain, although there were many ex-US Army trucks purchased by private operators after the end of the War. The handsome lines of the radiator, bonnet and cab of this 3 ton Austin K2 dropside lorry are typical. Factory fitted items for the convenience or comfort of drivers were more or less unknown; there was only one windscreen wiper for instance, though the seats were leather. Advertising RAY o VITOL POULTRY FOOD on its wooden bodyside, BFX 392 is in the livery of Broadwey Flour Mills Ltd; telephone Upwey 205 in the days when most numbers had two or three digits and you dialled the operator to connect you. The name of the secretary of the company, P.H.Flint, is stencilled on the chassis. Photograph Graham Herbert courtesy Dorset History Centre.

Crowds gather to watch as fire destroys the Ritz Theatre at Weymouth on 13 April 1954. This elegant building, dating from 1908, was constructed mainly of timber and it took a little over an hour for much of it to be destroyed. It had been undergoing refurbishment prior to the blaze and it was disclosed later that an errant blowlamp had been the cause of the fire. A new theatre was opened in 1960. Carriages stabled at the quay station can be glimpsed on the far right. Photograph Graham Herbert courtesy Dorset History Centre.

Above. This will be early morning as there are no dock workers in sight as a convoy of Adam Lythgoe lorries await loading with basic slag from the vessel *Rian* moored alongside the cargo stage on 24 October 1954. The lorries would be preservation items today; the leading vehicle is a Dodge followed by a Ford Thames Trader and an S type Bedford. Adam Lythgoe Ltd started trading in 1911 as agricultural merchants supplying farmers in the North West of England, before branching out into quarrying, supplying and spreading various grades of farm lime. The lorries in this view came from North Barn Quarry, Long Bredy near Bridport, and though no longer involved with quarrying the company is still in operation today as Adam Lythgoe (Estates) Ltd based in Widnes, Cheshire. The skeletal remains of the Ritz theatre destroyed by fire on 13 April 1954 can be seen in the background. The cargo stage went through a period of reconstruction beginning in September 1948 and completed in July 1951; the electric cranes date from that period. Photograph Graham Herbert courtesy Dorset History Centre.

Left. As one man directs the crane operator, two others gingerly guide a heavy 20 ton drum of Pirelli General 11,000 volt electricity cable into what looks to be some kind of landing craft. Photograph Graham Herbert courtesy Dorset History Centre.

A new forward control 1¼ ton Commer delivery van JJT 467 owned by J.H. Northover & Sons Ltd Groceries and Provisions, Weymouth. Photograph Graham Herbert courtesy Dorset History Centre.

A renowned sculptor and painter, Elizabeth Muntz, organised summer schools at the studio in her home, Apple Tree Cottage at East Chaldon, Dorset for young people developing their skills in painting, pottery and sculpture. A class is in progress in the picturesque setting overlooking the sea at East Chaldon on 1 October 1955. At left is her pony *Merrylegs* and her beloved Springer Spaniel *Rumple* can be glimpsed on the right below the easel. Her work won world wide recognition; the stone effigy of King Harold in Waltham Abbey, Griffins for the entrance gates at Lulworth Manor, and lead candlesticks for Eric Kennington's effigy of Lawrence of Arabia in St Martins Church, Wareham are just a few of her notable achievements, but her most unusual commission was the sculpture acknowledging *Simon* the ships cat of HMS *Amethyst*. The ship was bombarded by Chinese Communist gun batteries in the Yangtse River in 1949. Simon was wounded in the attack but survived; he raised the morale of the crew and was awarded the Dickin Medal, the animal equivalent of the VC for gallantry under enemy fire, he was also awarded the Blue Cross Medal. Photograph Graham Herbert courtesy Dorset History Centre.

A summer traffic jam in St Thomas Street with buses causing problems for motorists or is it the other way round? A line of cars including a Ford 100E with the interesting registration of PEA 943 are snaking around a parked double decker bus working service No.24. The Hillman parked outside Edwin Jones on the right is halting progress for the oncoming single deck bus working route No.228. Photograph Graham Herbert courtesy Dorset History Centre.

The beach is packed at the Southern end of the esplanade; note the waiting shelters which allowed double-parking of buses without hindrance to other vehicles. Photograph Graham Herbert courtesy Dorset History Centre.

The man who started it all. King George III changed the town's fortunes with his patronage and the grateful inhabitants erected the statue in 1810 to mark the 50th year of his reign. The statue looks towards the Jubilee clock on the esplanade erected in 1887 to celebrate the 50th year of the reign of his granddaughter – Queen Victoria. Photograph Graham Herbert courtesy Dorset History Centre.

Weymouth has had a lifeboat station since 1869 when the town's first lifeboat *Agnes Harriet* was named in a ceremony held on the beach before a large crowd. In the harbour on 14 June 1958 is the *Frank Spiller Locke,* on the day she was officially named and dedicated. The boat replaced the *William* and *Clara Ryland*. The present day Severn Class boat has been on station since 2002. Since the lifeboat station opened in 1869 Weymouth lifeboats have launched approximately 1,700 times and saved over 800 lives in the treacherous waters around Portland Bill and the Dorset coast. Photograph Graham Herbert courtesy Dorset History Centre.

Holidaymakers having breakfasted and left their respective B&Bs swarm along the pavement at Frederick Place beside the well-known and popular Fortes ice cream parlour and restaurant, a magnet on hot summer days for lovers of all flavours of delicious ice cream. Another popular venue next door is Howleys toyshop where buckets and spades, beach balls, rubber rings and all types of toys for all ages are to be found. Fortes premises today belong to Wetherspoons trading as The William Henry pub. Howleys are open in Weymouth still, as popular as ever and as part of the Toymaster Group, with an extensive range of toys and model railways. Frederick Place itself is a Georgian Terrace built on what used to be the gardens of Gloucester Lodge owned by Prince William Henry, Duke of Gloucester and younger brother of King George III. Photograph Graham Herbert courtesy Dorset History Centre.

Probably more familiar to Londoners who used to feed pigeons in Trafalgar Square, a roadside trader selling bird food - in this case the birds are a little bigger - swans! Photograph Graham Herbert courtesy Dorset History Centre.

A crowded St Thomas street in 1964, the Fyffes banana lorry holding up traffic. By coincidence the registration numbers of the double decker buses are in order; the first bus on route 61A is LTA 944 and the following on route 273 is LTA 945. The oncoming car is a Morris CPG 128 closely followed by a Nash Metropolitan 750 CEH, an attractive car of the day as all were made in two-tone colours. They were priced at £713 for the hardtop version and £725 for the convertible. A cyclist who seems to be looking at something behind him instead of concentrating on what perils lie ahead is following the Nash. The lines of cars parked alongside the pavement include a couple of old-timers plus a Morris Oxford, Ford 100E and an Austin Somerset. Graham Herbert courtesy Dorset History Centre.

An array of well-remembered vessels moored in Weymouth harbour in October 1961. *Roebuck* on the right and her sister ship *Sambur* alongside the cargo stage on the left date from 1925 and were the only ships built for the GWR especially for cargo traffic. Both were used extensively on the Channel Island trade for which the 1960 inward goods tonnage from the islands comprised 50,859 tons and parcels 5,106 tons; goods outwards in the same year totalled 29,329 tons. *Sambur* was withdrawn in March 1964. *Roebuck* ultimately became the last GWR ship to serve Weymouth, surviving until 1965. Moored in line ahead of the *Sambur* are the passenger ferries used on services to the Channel Islands *Caesarea, St Patrick* and *Sarnia*. Car ferries were introduced from Weymouth in 1973 and Hydrofoils took over from the 1980s. Unfortunately due to a defect found in the quay all sailings from Weymouth to the Channel Islands were transferred to Poole in 2012 albeit hopefully as a temporary measure. Photograph Graham Herbert courtesy Dorset History Centre.

Dick Emery
On location in Weymouth, 1965

Comic actor Dick Emery was one of the stars in what many consider to be the golden age of comedy on British television during the 1960s. *The Dick Emery Show* was the longest running sketch show on BBC TV with 166 episodes broadcast between 1963 and 1981. An audience of 17 million viewers made him the major star of BBC comedy. The characters created by Dick Emery are as well remembered today as they were all those years ago; who can forget – The Traffic Warden, Mandy, the Ton Up Boy, Bovver Boy, Gaylord, Hettie, Lampwick, Clarence, and many others. The following photographs date from 1965 when Dick Emery and his production team visited Weymouth to film his characters at various locations around the town.

Right. Dick Emery as the Traffic Warden, with another well known face from television, Deryck Guyler, on the streets of Weymouth in 1965. Dick played the warden perfectly, as the little man given a uniform plus a pencil and a notebook, the parking meter seems to be a prop as I am unable to recall seeing them at the time. Graham Herbert, courtesy Dorset History Centre.

Dick Emery on the far left in one of his many guises on the quayside opposite the Royal Oak Inn. The man holding the microphone is Deryck Guyler again, playing as usual the hapless interviewer of yet another Dick Emery creation. Note the onlookers, complete with a member of the Dorset Constabulary, cape folded neatly over left shoulder; *de rigueur* for policemen of this era. Luckily for the production team there are no trains passing along the tramway at this moment in the filming. Graham Herbert, courtesy Dorset History Centre.

Dick Emery as Mandy the brassy blonde with the famous catch phrase *Ooh you are awful* [pause] *but I like you* with Deryck Guyler during filming on Custom House Quay. Graham Herbert, courtesy Dorset History Centre.

The inevitable crowd observe the action with Dick Emery and Deryck Guyler on the Esplanade. Graham Herbert, courtesy Dorset History Centre.

Dick Emery brought most of his characters to the streets of Weymouth in 1965 and here is one of the most famous, Hetty the frustrated spinster, with Deryck Guyler the luckless interviewer. Graham Herbert, courtesy Dorset History Centre.

The location has now changed to the beach for a bevy of bathing belles. Part of the art deco Pier Bandstand dating from 1939 can be seen in the background. Graham Herbert, courtesy Dorset History Centre.

Appendices
Wish You Were Here!

November 1953: Dear M, B, G, N, C and dog. Back once again arriving at Reading station at 10.30. 72 miles door to door. Some fog here but not a problem. Calling at the butchers for Sunday joint. Don't forget it's a bank holiday.

July 1969: I will be able to come on the 25th all being well. Give my best wishes to him for a happy day. It's not quite so hot today. We had a nice holiday no rain but high winds some days. The West at its best.

WESTBURY WHITE HORSE.

29567

September 1959: Having a lovely time. Weather behaving fine and going to Frome for the weekend. I will be arriving home Monday and will see you Tuesday. J sends her regards.

The Market Square Frome from Bath Street – no message.

THE MARKET SQUARE FROM BATH STREET, FROME.

GEORGE HOTEL

August 1957: What a place this is. Having a great time walking. No rain which makes a change.

Market Square Frome – no message.

PARISH CHURCH FROM BIDES GARDENS.

MONTACUTE PRIORY.

PRINCES STREET.

YEOVIL

MIDDLE STREET AND GEORGE HOTEL.

THE BOROUGH.

August 1954: Having a holiday down here. Came by road and wished we hadn't. Where are your rich people going this year Timbucktoo?!!!! Haven't had any news from you lately. What's the idea!! How's your love life? Good I hope!! Back next Wednesday.

April 1984: Had a lovely couple of days camping, now on our way home. Thought I'd post this before we got there!

WEST BAY

SOUTH STREET

BRIDPORT & WEST BAY

WEST STREET

PARISH CHURCH

13 June 1928: We arrived safely and comfortably and having a fine time. Will write later and tell you where we have been. Weather not too bad. Where I have put the arrow, opposite the statue, we have a view of cliffs from our bedroom window. Hope you are well.

Esplanade and clock tower, Weymouth – no message.

We are getting younger every Day at
WEYMOUTH

BABY

We're too busy you'll see
To send any news,
But by lifting the flap,
You'll find all the Views

Left. 11 June 1928: Thought you'd like this. Having a lovely time love Leslie.

Below. 12 July 1973: Having a heavenly, lazy holiday. Weather smashing. We are getting to the stage where we are having to cover up a bit to save excess burning. Even Tony has been in the water this year. It is so clear in comparison to near us. You can see the bottom!

GREETINGS FROM WEYMOUTH

148

BRITISH RAILWAYS
Southern Region
DISTRICT TRAFFIC SUPERINTENDENT'S OFFICE
SOUTHAMPTON CENTRAL.

SPECIAL CIRCULAR NO. 4203.

My ref: R. 116220

13th May, 1961.

WEYMOUTH TRAMWAY AND PIER LINE.

The instructions under the above heading on pages 225 to 227
inclusive of the Western Section Appendix to the Working Timetable and
Books of Rules and Regulations are hereby suspended until further notice
and the working of the Tramway line must be carried out in accordance with
the following instructions.

DRAFT TO BE WORKED TO

WEYMOUTH TRAMWAY AND PIER LINE.

The Weymouth Tramway line extends from a junction with the
Portland Line at Weymouth to the gates at the entrance to the Quay, on
public thoroughfare and wharves. Various sidings lead from the Tramway.

The working of traffic over the Tramway is controlled by the Yard
Inspector or Foreman at Weymouth Station. On each occasion when an engine
or train is already on the Tramway the Yard Inspector or Foreman must so
advise the Shunter in charge of all other engines or trains proceeding to
the Quay.

The following instructions will apply to all trains and light
engines.

Two Shunters, (one of whom is referred to hereafter as the
"Shunter-in-Charge") working under the supervision of the Yard Inspector
or Foreman, must precede or accompany each engine or train working over
the Tramway, and no Driver must move his engine without being so
accompanied. The Shunter-in-Charge will be responsible for the direction
and safety of the movement. The second Shunter must act in accordance
with instructions from the Shunter-in-Charge.

The greatest care must be exercised by the enginemen and shunters
to guard against accidents, and ensure the safety of the public; and the
Driver must obey all signals and instructions given by the Shunters.

Head and tail lamps must be used on all trains and light engines
running over the Tramway.

Each engine working over the Tramway is provided with a bell
which the Fireman must ring continuously while the train or engine is in
motion at any point between the Weymouth Goods Yard entrance and Weymouth
Quay.

The speed of trains or engines must not exceed 4 miles per hour,
except as shown below, and must travel at a lower speed where necessary
to ensure safety.

Catch points are provided in the sidings connected with the
Tramway, and the points leading into the sidings are normally set for the
running line. The Shunter-in-Charge, who is responsible for the custody
of the loose levers provided to work the points, must have two in his
possession when travelling with a train over the Tramway, and must work
the points as necessary.

Wagons must not be coupled or uncoupled in motion on the Tramway
or in sidings.

PADDINGTON to WEYMOUTH
TRAIN FORMATIONS
From the Passenger Train Working at Paddington Station
Monday 14 June to 19 September (inc.), 1954.

Weekday Services;

08.20 (SX) Paddington to Weymouth Quay (will not run on Saturday, 18 September).
Saturdays excepted; Empty coaching stock to leave Old Oak Common at 07.20 for platform 3.
Train formation; Brake Compo, Dining Car (both to be detached at Weymouth Jct.). Van 3rd, 2 Thirds, 3 Compos, 2 Thirds, Van 3rd all for Weymouth Quay.
Train calling at; Reading General to pick up only, Westbury, Yeovil & Weymouth. .

08.20 (SO) Paddington to Weymouth Quay
Saturdays only; Empty coaching stock to leave Old Oak Common at 07.20 for platform 3.
Train formation; Van 3rd, 3 Thirds, Compo, Diner, Compo, 3 Thirds, Van 3rd all for Weymouth Quay.

08.30 (SO) Paddington to Weymouth Quay
Saturdays only; Empty coaching stock to leave Old Oak Common at 07.30 for platform 4.
Train formation; Brake Compo, Dining Car both to be detached at Weymouth Jct., Van 3rd, 2 Thirds, 3 Compos, 2 Thirds, Van 3rd all for Weymouth Quay.
Train calling at; Reading General (pick up only) and Weymouth.

On Saturdays, passengers for the Westbury and Weymouth Line advised to travel by the 09.35 Paddington to Minehead calling at Westbury.

12.30 Paddington to Weymouth Town
Empty coaching stock to leave Old Oak Common at 11.30 for platform 2.
Train formation; Van 3rd, 3rd, Compo, 3rd, Van 3rd all for Weymouth, 3rd Weymouth WFSO, Brake Compo Frome MTThO, Dining Car & Brake Compo both to be detached at Westbury.
Train calling at; Reading General, Newbury, Lavington, Westbury, Frome, Castle Cary, Yeovil Pen Mill, Maiden Newton, Dorchester West & Weymouth. *Calls at Sparkford to set down on notice being given to the guard at Castle Cary.*

18.00 Paddington to Weymouth Town
Empty Coaching stock to leave Old Oak Common at 17.00 for platform 4.
Train formation; Van 3rd, 3rd, Diner, Compo, Van 3rd all for Weymouth Town, 2 Thirds, Brake Compo all for Weymouth Quay on Saturdays; 3, 17, 24, 31 July & 7 August only. 3rd (WFO), Van 3rd, 1st (8), 3rd, Van 3rd to be detached at Newbury to form 19.18 to Trowbridge.
Two blank doors to be placed in rear Weymouth van Third.
Train calling at; Newbury, Hungerford, Bedwyn, Savernake (LL), Pewsey, Lavington, Westbury, Frome, Castle Cary, Yeovil Pen Mill, Maiden Newton, Dorchester West & Weymouth.
On Saturday, 3 July, also 17 July to 7 August (inclusive) will convey passengers for Weymouth Quay (for Channel Islands).

Trains conveying slip coaches for Weymouth and Slipped at Heywood Road Junction, Westbury.;

10.30 (SX) Paddington to Penzance – Cornish Riviera Express
Empty coaching stock to leave Old Oak Common at 09.25 and run via No.2 Carriage line from Subway Junction for platform 2.
Train formation; Van 3rd, 4 Thirds, 3rd Dining Saloon, Kitchen 1st, 1st (7), Compo, Van 3rd all for Penzance, 3rd & Brake Compo for Plymouth North Road, Slip for Westbury.

15.30 Paddington to Penzance
Empty coaching stock to leave Old Oak Common at 14.30 for platform 1.
Train formation; Van 3rd, 2 Thirds, Compo, Van 3rd, 3rd (SO), Brake Compo (SO) all for Penzance, Dining Car & Brake Compo for Plymouth, Brake Compo, Compo, 3rd, Van 3rd all (SX) for Kingswear, Slip, Compo (FO) & 3rd (SO) all for Weymouth.

The 10.30 ex Paddington ceased slip-workng at Heywood Road Junction in September 1958 and the 15.30 slip service was withdrawn from January 1959.

Working Freight Timetable Winter 1957-Western Region
Freight Trains for Weymouth Line

Down
04.00 Westbury-Weymouth-Continuation of 22.40 ex Paddington Sat. (MO)
05.10 Bristol East Depot-Weymouth (MOQ)
05.50 Rogerstone-Weymouth (Loco Coal) (MO)
06.25 Westbury-Yeovil Junction (Loco Coal) (MX)
06.50 Westbury-Weymouth (SO) Milk Empties
08.10 Westbury-Sparkford (SX)
08.40 Bristol East Depot-Weymouth (MX)
10.40 Westbury-Weymouth (Q)
11.45 Severn Tunnel Jcn-Weymouth
11.49 Upwey-Weymouth
12.55 Yeovil Pen Mill-Weymouth (SX)
13.20 Swindon-Weymouth
13.20 Bristol-Weymouth (MX)
18.35 Bristol East Depot-Weymouth (SO)
21.00 Westbury-Yeovil Pen Mill (SX)
22.40 Paddington-Weymouth (MX)

Up Trains
01.50 Weymouth-Avonmouth Dock (MX)
04.30 Weymouth-Avonmouth Empties (MXQ)
06.45 Weymouth-Cardiff Empties
09.37 Weymouth-Yeovil Pen Mill (SX)
11.00 Weymouth-Upwey (SX)
11.45 Sparkford-Westbury (SX)
13.48 Weymouth-Rogerstone Empties
18.15 Yeovil-Cardiff Parcels
18.20 Yeovil (Hendford)-Westbury (SX)
18.35 Weymouth-Paddington Milk
19.55 Weymouth-Bristol
22.30 Weymouth-Bristol East Depot (SO)

MO Mondays only
MX Mondays Excepted
SX Saturdays excepted
Q Runs when required
SO Saturdays Only

850 LORD NELSON after arrival at Weymouth with a train from Bournemouth in 1948. A.E. West, courtesy Mike King.

5975 WINSLOW HALL freshly coaled and with plenty of steam to spare, is ready to be turned before working from Weymouth to her home shed at Westbury in 1957. A.E. West, courtesy Mike King.